A WICCAN BARDO

A WICCAN BARDO

INITIATION AND SELF-TRANSFORMATION

by

REV. PAUL V. BEYERL

PRISM · UNITY

The author acknowledges the use of *The Charge of the Goddess* and *The Witches' Rune* by Doreen Valiente.

Published in 1989 by

PRISM PRESS
2 South Street
Bridport
Dorset DT6 3NQ

and distributed in the USA by

AVERY PUBLISHING GROUP INC.
350 Thorens Avenue
Garden City Park
New York 11040

and published in Australia 1989 by

UNITY PRESS
6a Ortona Road
Lindfield
NSW 2070

1 85327 036 9

Printed and bound in the Channel Islands
by The Guernsey Press Limited

Contents

I have felt the desire for several years to write this book. If I look into my soul, that compulsion is as old as this incarnation — most likely far more ancient. For my inspiration, I dedicate this book to those who follow the Tradition of Lothlorien; to my acolyte Lawrence; to friends Dawn Heather and Donna Lyon Rhose, and to my partner, Larry Pascoe.

Chapter I
Wicca — A Journey Twice Taken

Having attained my forties, I am old enough to have learned that growth is continual, that the pursuit of wisdom is an ultimate joy, that Union with the Universe brings ecstasy. I am also old enough to have enjoyed the fruits reaped of past lessons. I have gone in Circles long enough to know that life moves in cycles. The journey which I have taken in this Wiccan life is a journey taken before. It builds upon the training and experiences gleaned living a Lama's difficult existence in the Himalayan Mountains. It echoes the herbal experience I practised as a rotund midwife in an African village which was doomed to destruction. It studies anew the struggle with the establishment of church bureaucracy and issues of personal integrity I encountered as a Roman Catholic prelate. This journey has brought me back to Paracelsus, to the teachings of both Buddha and Christ, and this journey I willingly take again, moving into a New Age and creating a new Wiccan Tradition to leave as imprints of my aging feet as they walk humbly into the cauldron of memory and rebirth.

But even more, this Wiccan life has brought me back to the Earth. It has been this Earth which, in all my lives, has been the thread of continuity as I take pleasure in the cycles of rebirth. It is upon this planet we are born into physical bodies which enable our spiritual selves to explore sensate manifestation, to move beyond the Bardo realm of unbridled imagination. If we see our planet as the manifest reality of Mother Nature, Goddess of Fertility, then surely this Earth is the jewel of Her web. As young as I can remember, my religious training held that God is everywhere. Having spent my life time searching for an understanding of the nature of what that religion called God, I have found that lesson indisputable. What our Western cultures call God is truly everywhere and is within every thing.

The word God has come to represent an anthropomorphic, male representation of the all-pervasive power of the Universe. This is difficult to translate into another of those great lessons I learned as a child. In my early Saturday morning catechisms I was taught that we are made in the image of God. But we are made in multi-faceted images. We are not all male by any means. We are not all Caucasian. Nor are we even all heterosexual. While the creation of an image for God becomes necessary when one desires to communicate with the Universe or to relate to that Divine Power it should never be so limited as to be inaccessible to so many.

Throughout all of human history, not excluding modern, mainstream traditional religions, we also create God in our images. The process of establishing images of creation for the definition and experience of another's reality is Magick. Magick is the product of imagination when integrated with simple but essential disciplines. It would be fair to say that between God and humankind there has been mutual magick throughout many Ages.

As one devoted to the Earth, I became increasingly uncomfortable with the singular nature of God. As I moved through my Wiccan training, there was a gradual process of accepting the concept of Goddess, for the Moon's pervasive power and the birthing of flowers in the Spring, the mothers and daughters of our reality all testify that the feminine aspect of the Divine Universe is alive and thriving. Perhaps it was not chance at all which birthed me into this life, into my first temple, a nursery painted blue by parents who had me dedicated to Christ's mother, Mary, who some theologians perceive as an archetype of the Goddess. These words, God and Goddess, are but symbols and it is essential to be ever-mindful that They are but representations of a human's conceptualization for the two primary polarities of the Universe. They are no more human than are the archetypes of Yin and Yang.

Similarly, there are numerous symbols and archetypes available to the modern neo-pagan communities. Many of these have historical roots but, because we are not literally bound by our symbols, we have the freedom to be creative and child like, restrained only by the limitations of our own doubts and inhibitions. The neo-pagan and Wiccan religions now in existence are in a remarkable position, for they are creating their own religions. What is religion? It is any system which seeks to provide an understanding of the Universe. Religion enables the individual to hold a personal relationship and communicate with that Universe (some would say with God).

I am a Wiccan Priest. It is who I am, first, foremost and at all hours of every day. By definition, this means that I am a Witch, yet I use that word with great discretion. Some would have neo-pagans and Wiccans avoid use of the word Witch altogether, for fear of contamination with the perverted and inaccurate meanings which permeate the beliefs of certain other religions and infect the media. Although I may be discreet in my use of the word, I cannot remove it from usage. It is a sacred identity and links me to another past life in which I was persecuted to the point of death for beliefs which were called evil during the years of the witchcraft trials. It has taken years of training, of study, of learning discipline to truly become a Witch. To me the word Witch is a special, private word. When pressed by those of mainstream religions, I explain the Reverend before my name as being multi-denominational. My Wiccan church, The Rowan Tree, includes members who are primarily neo-pagan, some of whom intensively study the Tradition of Lothlorien. Not all of our members fall into this category. We have a substantial portion of those who identify themselves as Christians, even those who work within Christian churches. We usually have representation also from Buddhist beliefs and we bring our denominations together, for we share the knowledge that symbols are but symbols.

There are many who call themselves Witches, but one must understand that there are as many types of Witches as there are

...s. Wiccan Traditions and sects can be as disparate as ...ptists are from the High Church of England, as the ...elicals are from the Scandinavian Lutherans. The di... ...ences between various Traditions may be perceived not only as differences in ethics, in the application of disciplines and practises, but also in the use of symbols as tools of Magick.

If there are two hundred thousand Witches in the world, then there are inevitably two hundred thousand types of Witchcraft. Being deeply religious all my life, it was an unfolding of lotus-born joy as Wicca brought me to self-actualization and a positive relationship with reality. Reality has brought me a commitment to the Mississippi River and her valleys. Because Wicca is not defined by an all pervasive dogma, as it is still evolving, it is taking many forms. More and more I have seen practitioners begin to better understand their natural environment, its patterns of weather, vegetation and of seasons. This information is balanced with research into the customs and beliefs of ancient cultures which lived in similar environments. When several Los Angeles Witches told me that their religion was becoming more and more modeled after the Mediterranean cultures, it spoke of this current evolution. Truly we have come a long way from the singular practises of the sixties and the common eclecticism of the seventies. Now we are truly developing Traditions capable of surviving into the future.

In addition, my Wiccan research has given me an understanding of the nature of the Universe itself which the newest scientific discoveries only confirm. We know that our Sun will slowly expire, victimized by the very life-giving radiant light which enables us to exist. The ancient myths in which the god inevitably trades his life for the lives of those he supports are consistent with the solar system as we know it. Ultimately, even the Universe itself plays out the perpetual dance of birth and death and rebirth. We are currently living in that stage of the Universe's life which is between birth and death. Stars complete their life cycles and collapse. Astronomers scan the heavens and record these events. As the cauldron of the Universe becomes more populous with black holes increasing in matter and energy, eventually their intensity will become too strong and, unable to contain themselves any longer, will release a tremendous explosion of matter and energy, shaking the foundations of all reality. As those bits of creativeness are scattered throughout infinity, cool, and begin to contain lifeforms, sooner or later someone will describe that big bang as the creative voice of the Divine. The genesis of reality is described in strikingly similar myths in a great many religions. When looked at objectively, (from the mountain, Confucious would recommend), they tell the same story of reality's nature which science seeks to ascertain. Existence is a constant cycle of death and rebirth which neither our planet nor solar system may escape.

Although modern Wicca is very young, younger than some of its myths of ancient heritages and traditions would have us believe, we must look deeply at the theology of that which we espouse. It is important to better understand the implications of our religious practises. And it is important to establish the foundations of all Traditions so that they are prepared for and can withstand the onset of future time.

Current practises assure us that the future of civilization faces frightening challenges. We live in an era which has been very indulgent. There has been an abundance available to the common individual which is unparalleled in times past and remains unfound in the poor regions of our planet. In order to preserve the Earth in a reasonable condition and avoid the changes which loom before us, all races and peoples must embrace a level of change so drastic most of civilization finds it unacceptable. Avoidance of those changes will bring dire consequences, indeed.

I love this planet and I love the life forms which inhabit Her, plant and animal alike. But I cannot work to preserve humanity at the imperilment of the Earth, for without Her there will no longer be human life. One of the functions common to many Wiccan Traditions is the commitment to assist the Earth through this time of change. Not only do groups reach out to embrace the entire sphere of our Earth, but we also are deeply committed on a local level. It is not by accident that the Deva Ritual of Lothlorien is set on the sandy shores of a sacred river, deep within a glade, for that is the Mothervalley of the Mississippi as found in my homeland, the source of this great river. This is not the first life I have spent upon a primary river. Even in this life as a child I would find water with a forked willow cut by my father from our family tree. Although I left dowsing behind in my childhood, the quest for water eventually brought me to the Mississippi. Lush, green, fertile, I do not like the thought of this river passing south though an arid country turned desert, all topsoil blown away in the wind. Current ecological trends indicate that at some not-too-distant future time, this beloved, fertile valley which begins in Minnesota, may mark the southern edge of the crop-growing area of North America. What this speaks of our modern trends ought be alarming to practitioners of Earth religions world-wide.

We Witches speak about reincarnating with our current friends and neo-pagan peers. Wiccan religion does hold the keys to success in such an endeavor, but such a feat of magick is not automatically inherent in our system. The exemplary role models found high in the Himalayan Mountains clearly show us the need to take our religious disciplines more seriously than we do and carefully establish the necessary symbolic tools in order to truly reincarnate and reclaim an athame or any other physical tool used in this current life.

But in such discussions I can only speak for myself and must speak through the type of Wicca which I practise and which I live. This book will take you on a mental journey through the heart of that Wiccan Tradition which I founded for those who have been and for those who remain my students. It is impossible to discuss the nature of Wiccan theology without a thorough look at ritual, for ritual is where we bring our beliefs into manifestation. Ritual is the process through which we exemplify our theology. But ritual itself is easily misunderstood.

In the mastery of ritual, one is no longer self-conscious. One is aware solely of one's spiritual essence. That mastery, however, is a sought-after ideal and is not to imply that such a transcendental state is easily achieved. Ritual provides a cautious means through which we reconstruct the Universe on a microcosmic level, intimate enough to fit within one's temple. Through the archetypes and symbols which are the stones and mortar of this creation do we extend consciousness and become One with the Divine. The rituals of this book may deal with a variety of social situations, such as marriage or even death, but the nature of the Universe and the Wiccan theology being implemented remains constant. It is my goal to use various rituals to discuss modern Wiccan theology.

One of the reasons I began to create a new Tradition was due to the poetic nature of my soul. The Book of Shadows I wrote for my students waxes very poetic. At times students have questioned the profusion of poetic beauty in the Tradition of Lothlorien. There is something nostalgic and intrinsically romantic about calling upon four Unicorns as representatives of the four classical manifest elements. Oh, to be sure, there is also a Unicorn for the fifth element of spirit. Among Rowan Tree folk that Unicorn is known as Andrius.

Some students are anxious to get into serious religious study and intensive ritual disciplines and have asked when the Book of Shadows puts away its rose-coloured glasses. Although the poetry is very emotionally moving, it can also be misleading. One must look through the poetic prose. Poetry is merely a two dimensional image: the art, through which one must look to see the Universe. It becomes three dimensional when the images exist within one's mind. Those Unicorns which inhabit the realms of Lothlorien are every bit as serious and effectual as the Four Winds are to a Native Shaman or as the Four Archangels are to a Ceremonial Practitioner. The adoption of Unicorns both connects us with these long-standing archetypes, yet also provides us freedom from our past and the impetus to create our future. Newly created astral archetypes, when based upon sound, traditional forms, are every bit as effective and powerful.

By using such poetic, uplifting text in our Book of Shadows the student has access to spiritual aspiration, for the poetry uplifts and carries one through difficult times. Those who pursue the study of Wicca or that of Magick will find difficult times before them, for Magick is change and change is something Western society does not teach us to embrace. Magick is also the process through which one makes dreams become manifest. My Christian heritage suggests that we were once a dream in the mind of God. A major school of philosophical thought maintains that our future is determined by the self as it desires and wishes. It could be said that we dream our future, not only while asleep but at all moments of our lives. The portions of the Book of Shadows of Lothlorien contained in this text demonstrate but one manner in which one Tradition of Wiccan theology is used to dream its future.

The decision to open major portions of our Book of Shadows has not been made lightly. We maintain the old-fashioned virtues of secrecy. Indeed, even within our Wiccan church, students of the Mysteries must be silent about their studies until attaining the necessary skills and disciplines. Then they perform a yogic ritual form, announcing to our community that they pursue both initiation and ministry. Not only is this a debut performance but it opens them to scrutiny from the other members of both the Church and the Mystery School.

This book does not desire to espouse one Tradition over others. Rather I ask that you read it as a study of Wiccan theology. As neo-paganism and Wiccan religions grow, they will surely become established and respectable, if not populous. A discussion of theology needs reference material and I must use that with which I am most familiar. It is the intimacy of familiarity which assure me that this journey I take through Wicca is not new. I suspect the same is true for many people who find Wicca stirs vestiges of beliefs, traces of religions both Piscean and tribal. Such experience may well be a contributing factor for much of the myth-making of ancient sources for modern creations. Wicca, for me, is an experience as if every journey of my past is being retaken.

Chapter II
The Ritual Of Lothlorien

Ritual is an art form. The performance of ritual is a discipline drawing upon a variety of skills. The discipline of motion, grace made manifest, as studied by the student of Tai Ch'i is essential. One draws upon the beauty of dance and the power of the dancer. A vast history of ritual theatre and even of modern theatrical technique would be of great value. Ritual is an art, but it is also the study of a form.

In the Lamaist Traditions of Tibet, the Circle is worked through the various mandalas which one learns as progression is made through initiatory pathworking. The word yoga is generally believed to be derived from the Sanskrit term which means to yoke. The form of ritual worked in the Tradition of Lothlorien is one in which we yoke ourselves to the basic, primal nature of the Universe and invoke the awesome beauty of creativity.

The Ritual of Lothlorien is our basic ritual form or structure. Most other rituals which the Novice will later encounter follow the same form. This Ritual may also be used to work within the astral temple which is described within THE HOLY BOOKS OF THE DEVAS. Within the advanced levels of The Mystery School, The Ritual of Lothlorien is used within a more complex & challenging astral temple. Within the outer circles this Ritual is used to gather and focus our concentration in order to channel group energies in a cohesive manner.

By recreating the creation myth common to many religions and many eras, one is replicating the nature of the Divine and the Nature of the Universe. Ritual is the means by which we yoke ourselves to the Universe and to our beloved Earth as the manifest reality of God/dess. This form requires steady concentration and the ability to blend that skill with the arts of ritual theatre. It is essential that the mind not give way to the heart, for although the poetry is moving and the imagery lovely, discipline is what brings forth the Magick.

The yoking which takes place in the Ritual of Lothlorien is that of a Magick closely associated with the Mothervalley, the fecund, lush valley of the Mississippi River, which I cannot but think of as feminine (although it has been named by the pre-European residents as the Father of Waters). Part of a Priest/ess's training involves coming to understand the relationship between this river and the continent of North America. Through the magickal interaction of our Tradition and this river, we have the ability to embrace this entire continent.

There is a further, more serious consideration in yoking oneself to North America. With the upcoming climactic changes, the area in which we, here in Minneapolis, live will become the southern edge of the fertile lands. The increase in temperature throughout the globe, caused by a multitude of human sins, is such that the majority of what is now the United States will become arid and desertlike. There is a spiritual quality about the Mothervalley in this area. In part it can be traced to a deviation in gravity which is an anomaly, compared in studies to the similar deviations (caused by ancient flows of magma) located in the Andes and in the Himalayan Mountains. One cannot but speculate upon the future of a Mystery School in such a setting.

In the establishment of a ritual form designed to function as a yogic dance between Priest/ess and one's environment, any Tradition must come to terms with ecological responsibility, environmental protectionism, and a commitment to love and serve the local land. Local need not be defined in miles, for one can also develop an intimate relationship with the globe, itself, and relate to the entire planet in such a manner. But the energy of the land where one lives is inevitably drawn into the Circle. Careful awareness ought be given to one's local Magick. The weather, the climate, the changes in the seasons, the patterns of the stars which dance above your latitude; all are works of Magick from a source far greater than any of us. We are merely taking the journey again, dancing the creative flow of the

Universe when we take our steps around the Magick Circle.

Casting The Circle

In order to set aside and establish the sacred space, the ritual athame (knife) is used. The Priest/ess begins in the East. As the athame is pointed towards the Eastern horizon, the power of the rising Sun is called forth. The mental image is of a band of golden flame given forth from the blade's tip. The knife is taken around past the South, where the Sun attains noon fullness and past the West where He descends at sunset. The Northern half of the Circle is a descent through the Land of Death: following sunset the Sun passes behind the Earth and is reborn again the next morning. In Lothlorien, the athame is taken a full Circle plus the quarter from East to South so that the scribing is completed at the point at which the Sun is at His zenith, shining forth in His maximum glory.

The outer edge of the blade carries within it the power to banish fear, for this journey also implies the symbolic death and rebirth of the self as emissary of the Sun. All other negative attitudes are also warded away from the Circle. A ritual knife is also a weapon, and that fierce image carries with it the power to banish those emotions, attitudes and energies which would inhibit the flow of joy and of positive power.

As the Priest/ess walks deosil (clockwise) to complete the Circle, the inner edge of the blade represents the cutting edge of one's word, not unlike the lightning which cuts through the darkened sky. This is the principle of Magick in which the Word is capable of putting manifestation into motion at the very beginning. Our ethics are intrinsically bonded in the saying that a Priest/ess is only as good as his/her word. It is this openness and honesty which metaphorically fills the sacred space with what might be described as ozone, or the etheric principle of the Earth sphere. Although we work a circle, the completed shape is actually that of a sphere. It would be appropriate to liken this to the metaphorical establishment of the firmament of the temple.

Next, the pair of generally white altar candles are lit. The altar is set North of the Circle's centre, for the North represents the element of Earth. In working with the I Ching, one faces North in order to address the Oracle and receive its wisdom. The left candle is lit first, representing the light of the Sun which is the primary source of energy for our planet. The flame is then carried to the right altar candle which represents the Moon. Is it not wonderful that these two sources of light, one so distant but dominant, the other so subtle yet so very close we might almost extend to Her our hand, appear to the eye to be of equal size? And for us, that equality teaches an important religious truth: if the Divine has truly created in its own image, then the Divine itself is a combination of the polarities.

A chalice of water has been waiting upon the altar. Generally, our Priest/esses take great delight in developing a personal ritual water. I collect water from sacred springs around the world, from the oceans, and directly from Mother Nature, Herself, when it rains. Water, however, is rarely pure, for it is a receptive element and will carry with it minerals or gasses, silt or pollution. For ritual work it will need to be purified. The chalice is held in one hand, and with the other the Priest/ess places the point of the athame into the water, chanting:

> Be gone all darkness, flee this chalice,
> Leave it free from evil malice.
> Fill it full with joy and love and
> Blessings from the Gods above.

The next element which will be introduced is that of Earth. Water and Earth are both receptive or feminine elements and will be mixed together to work as One. Salt has held ritual significance which dates back through the biblical Books of Genesis. It was valued for its natural ability to preserve and gained a reputation for purity. Salt was most commonly gathered from the oceans. Frequently, the Priest/ess will use seasalt to acknowledge this heritage. As a small bowl of salt is

14

taken from the altar, held forth and touched with the athame's point, the following is chanted:

> Salt of the Earth, Salt of the Sea,
>> Born of the pure, so Blessed Be!
> Water for bodies; Salt for the soul,
>> At home in our Mother, such is our goal.

The most obvious mixture of earth and water upon our planet is that of the mighty oceans, laced with salt. These two elements are reunited as the Priest/ess places three measures of salt into the chalice of water. As s/he walks around the altar to the East, a great event is about to take place. The Circle is aspurged, the Priest/ess moving deosil. Not only is the temple area being sprinkled with sacred waters, but this re-enacts the ancient myths in which the seas are created. By moving around the perimeter of the Circle, the temple becomes symbolic of land mass, for all the lands upon our planet are embraced and surrounded with salted waters. We aspurge the Circle and the Sea washes the perimeter of our homelands. No matter how distant the shores the oceans are ever-present.

In order for creation to continue, there must be those agents of life-giving substance before the Divine Spark comes forth. Without the fires of the forest there would be no ash to enrich the soil. Without the smoky outpouring of the volcano, there would be desert islands rather than lush tropical havens. These are the processes which are kept in mind as a block of glowing charcoal is placed into the censer and the Priest/ess's own herbal mixture is spooned atop the glowing ember. Air and Fire being active, life-giving forces, the chant calls upon the active, masculine half of the Universe in balance to what has just gone before:

> By fire and smoke do I invoke
> Our Father from above.
> Fill this rite with Your might,
> With sacredness and love.

The combined forces of fire and air, when brought together upon our Earth, may at times appear destructive in their aggressive nature, but they prepare the sacred places for that which the Mother will birth. Now is the Circle prepared for the gestation of Magick.

This is when guests or co-workers are welcomed into the Circle through a portal or imaginary opening in the Northeast corner. Once all have been brought in and concentration has been resumed, the will of the Circle is established. This is accomplished by introducing the power of the staff or wand. This ritual tool has an affinity with the nature of the Age of Aries and figures strongly in the religous histories of that era. As this tool is taken around (the same Circle plus a quarter as the athame) the temple, the collective mindset focuses with the sense of psychic control for those events which will be taking place. It is the presence of will and the discipline of control which enable visualization techniques to be successful. The future of any ritual working depends upon this skill. As this is done, the Priest/ess chants:

> Seal this Circle with our wands
> Dancing round-about.
> Keep all Magick here inside,
> Keep all evil out.

Invoking the Elements and Cardinal Watchtowers

If we gaze upon our temple, now, as a creative sphere in which life is about to gestate, it is appropriate to begin by bringing forth the astral forms of being. There are three complete sets of elemental invocations in The Ritual of Lothlorien. Although we consistently work the energy flow in the same direction, deosil starting with the East, the invocations are performed in a variety of manners. Each of the three East invocations may be performed, then the three for the South, and so forth. Often we will do one set of invocations before beginning the next. We have also been known to perform them simultaneously, creating a glorious sound which can only be creative. Before any astral forms are called forth, the four elements in their primal, basic state are invoked.

The first set of elemental invocations was originally written for the Ritual of First Degree Initiation. They were also included in The Deva Ritual (from THE HOLY BOOKS OF THE DEVAS) as the lessons which the Unicorns brought to the plant kingdom before the herbes were taken through death and rebirth at the loving hands of Mother Nature.

The Priest/ess gathers the flame from an altar candle and moves around the altar to the East. In the East is an incense burner and a yellow candle. S/he lights both and chants the invocation as the plumes of herbal smoke drift into the etheric realms:

> And the Goddess
> Breathed gently into the void;
> And behold, the gentle breezes
> Caressed the soul of the Universe.
> Thus was born the essence of light,
> Of laughter and cheer . . .
>
> Pan sat alone in the Mother's Woodland.
> Raising His pipes to His mouth
> He brought forth the first Music,
> The wings of song,
> Floating in the airs . . .
>
> May the gentle winds of faith
> Stir your soul into seeking the Mother.
> As the morning song of the dawning
> Creeps over the horizon of your life,
> May we all share in the laughing
> And joy of wisdom
> And may we float in
> The winged clouds of Eternity . . .

From the East, after time has passed for pondering these lovely words, the Priest/ess moves to the South. In the South is a red candle and a small firepot or cauldron. S/he pours fuel into the pot, sets it to flame and lights the candle. The invocation is read as the tongues of fire dance and flicker:

> From the warmth of
> Her maternal goodness
> Did She bring fire
> To Her children,
> To kindle in them the sparks of knowledge
> And the fires of delight . . .
>
> From the Sun we take our warmth;
> From our Mother comes desire.
> As the Phoenix rises
> Renewed of flames may we, too,
> Embrace the life beyond this . . .
>
> Our Eternal Goddess
> Is the Cauldron of Cerridwen;
> May we dance around Her fires
> In eternal joy . . .
> May we embrace
> The fires of learning
> And kindle within
> Our passion for wisdom . . .

In the West sits a small basin or receptacle, alongside it a small pitcher with ritual water. The Priest/ess lights the blue candle and pours the water into the basin. The sound dances into the holy sphere and fills the temple with its own Magick as s/he reads:

> From the deep waters
> Of Her eternal wisdom
> Brings She forth
> The Mystery of Life,
> And thus does the Initiate
> Take on the Quest of All-Knowing . . .

From the Cauldron of Cerridwen
We take compassion and love.
Moving deep within the Mysteries
We seek inner knowledge . . .
May the God Neptune watch over the Seeker
As the Initiate plunges into the depths of knowing . . .

Our Mother is
The Moon's reflection upon rippling waters . . .
May we eternally be bathed
In Her love . . .
May we seek Her calm,
Her tranquility,
As we travel from shore
To distant shore . . .

The flame is carried around to the North. There waits a pot of earth, of soil gathered from many sacred sites and sacred Circles, with a few gems, crystals, perhaps with sand from the pyramids or ash from volcanoes. The green candle is lit and the Priest/ess slowly sinks the ritual athame into the soil. This gesture reminds us of the original consecration of this sacred blade, in which it was buried in the Earth to bind us to our sacred oaths of conservation and preservation. As this is done, the invocation is chanted:

In our quest for knowledge
We cross the fields of the Earth Mother
And play in Her forests . . .
Her pulse is in the gardens,
Her dance is in the jungles and from deep within Her
Springs knowledge as the fruits of the Earth . . .

Slowly She dances the seasonal rhythms,
To the gentle music of the Woodlands.
Pan plays upon His pipes,
And She dances in the grasses,
Among the trees,

To the tune of the Gentle Hunter . . .

Our Mother is the Earth and we are Her children:
She gives us wisdom.
May we seek Her knowledge in the flowers
And in the green things . . .
And in the passing of time
When we give to Her our souls,
She will take our bodies
And plant them for her flowers . . .

The second set of elemental invocations calls upon the Mother of Nature in Her elemental forms, moving through air, through fire and water, and through earth, to begin the process of making spirit manifest, of bringing forth life and Magick. Sometimes we chant them, intoning long notes and moving together through the words. Sometimes they are sung with the melodies I created in 1987, nearly ten years after their inception (see the appendices). In the Deva Ritual, they are sung by each of the elemental Unicorns to the Goddess, as they bow in Her honor:

To the East

O Beautiful Lady,
Gentle Goddess fair;
Give to us Thy wisdom,
Fill us with Thine air!

Bring to us Thy wondrous might,
Gracious Goddess of the light;
Ride the wings of Raphael
And bless this Magick rite!

Help us cast this Circle
And build a Magick Ring!
Guide us to Your beauty,
Our love to You we sing!

Goddess of the dawning light,

Kiss the dew of morning's sight,
Light the candle, ring the bell
And bless this Magick Rite!

To the South
Greatest Goddess of the fire
Fill my heart with Your desire;
Keep my feet upon Thy path
Fill my heart with mirth and laugh!

Greatest Goddess, burning bright,
Keep me in Thy magick might;
Dance around the fire bright,
Chant the song and do the rite.

Fire burning, fire bright,
Give my soul your magick light;
Help me rise anew each day,
Keep me in our Lady's way.

To the West
Queen of the Waters,
    sparkling in the moonlight;
Lady of the Heavens,
    dancing in the stars bright;

Dance in the laughing waves,
    call upon the Moon,
Cast the Circle, chant the song,
    Goddess, grant this boon!

Take us to Thy homeland,
    deep within the sea,
Bring the Moon into my heart,
    Dear Mother, Blessed Be!

Dance in the laughing waves
    call upon the Moon,
Cast the Circle, chant the song,
    Goddess, grant this boon!

To the North
Walking on the Earth this day,
Sensing life within;
Living with the Goddess' song,
We are free from sin!

Dancing in the forest,
Chanting with the trees;
Casting Magick Circles,
Singing Blessed Be's!'

Mother of the harvest,
Goddess of the fields;
You Who bring our dreams to ripe,
You Who bless the yields:

Join us dancing in the wood,
Hear us singing to the trees,
Help us cast our Circle,
Hear our Blessed Be's!'

'But what about the stars?' asks the Little Unicorn in one of our Yule rituals. The scribing of pentagrams is common to most Wiccan traditions. This represents the calling upon the Watchtowers which, to us, represent the spiritual guardian energies of our Circle. Each of the four invocations limns the imagery representing the power behind the symbol of the pentagram. The symbols which create the fabric's web are gathered from a variety of Traditional sources. Within Lothlorien they may be used to call upon a more traditional form of Watchtower, but may also be used to call upon the four Unicorns which were given life in the Deva Ritual.

Of any of the work done invoking elemental energy, this requires the greatest mental focus. This is when the work of the collective visualizations is set forth to invoke the actual power which resides within the archetypical element. Some individuals may establish visualizations of specific facets of the collected symbols for each quarter, others may be creating a larger fabric. However, all present direct their images through the Priest/ess, who channels them into the athame and through the blade as each pentagram is scribed.

Moving to the East, the Priest/ess stands in careful concentration, athame poised to begin the work of art as the words are intoned:

> Lords of the East, creatures of Air,
> Come, watch this rite, bring blessings fair!
> Sylphs and swords and dawn's fair light,
> Where the rainbow's born,
> Raphael, on Eurus' breath,
> Will ride the wings of morn.

Invoking Air Pentagram

> Lords of the East, creatures of Air,
> Come, watch this rite, bring blessings fair!

Building upon the first element, the level of intensity may actually be felt to increase as the Priest/ess walks around to the South quarter for the next invocation:

> Lords of the South, creatures of Fire,
> Come, watch this rite, bring us desire!
> Salamanders of the South,
> Notus' fiery breath;
> Living under Michael's care
> Rebirth follows death.

Invoking Fire Pentagram

Lords of the South, creatures of Fire,
Come, watch this rite, bring us desire!

To a great extent, the Priest/ess also channels each of the elements, or may be perceived as embodying those properties as each element is brought forth:

Lords of the West, creatures of Seas,
Come, watch this rite, fill it with ease!
Creatures of the moonlit sea,
Zephrus, Undines, all!
Drink with love from Gabriel's cup,
Hear the Goddess' call.

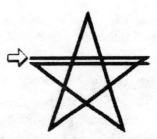

Invoking Water Pentagram

Lords of the West, creatures of Seas,
Come, watch this rite, fill it with ease!

Another significant aspect of these invocations is that they represent a collection of imagery common to the community. In establishing group workings, it is important to realize that having a common vocabulary of symbols and placement of images is a priority. Personal preferences of images and their placement must be secondary.

> Lords of the North, creatures of Earth,
> Come, watch this rite, fill it with mirth!
> Gnomes and Dryads, stones and trees,
> Pentacles and Boreas' strength;
> Auriel sends us wintertime
> And nights of growing length.

Invoking Earth Pentagram

> Lords of the North, creatures of Earth,
> Come, watch this rite, fill it with mirth!

Empowering the Circle

At this point, all of the formal preparations have been made to establish the sacred space into which the creative spark of life is to be brought. The Circle has been cleansed and scribed, and the elements brought forth in balance. The introduction of astral life, of the sentient energy of the astral Watchtowers, allows the Priest/ess to communicate with the

Circle in a more direct manner than any Novice can understand. Yet this Circle is a creation out of our collective psyches. Although very real, it is a function of our individual and collective minds. As such, it will be whatever we expect it to be. This implies a most serious sense of responsibility, one which can only be taken with great care. As a result, the next step in the ritual form is to deliver a Charge to the Circle. This may be considered both literal and symbolic. The Priest/ess takes up the ritual sword. In our Tradition this tool represents similar virtues as the athame, but magnified to represent the intent of all who attend the ritual itself, plus the values of our church and our community. It is for this reason that, within Lothlorien, the sword is a tool associated with the Second Degree Initiate, or that of Ministry.

The Priest/ess holds the sword and faces the point at which the scribing was begun. As the spiral route of the athame is retraced, the Circle is given instruction to represent a place of Perfect Love and Perfect Trust, so filled with controlled, positive energy that there will be no room for any negative energy. The Circle is empowered to become a sphere, representing the Womb of Creation and a place where the Divine Polarities may be brought into union.

Invoking the Goddess

The energy which represents the Goddess is brought into the Circle (traditionally) through the channel of a Priestess. There are other times when we might gather in a Circle, seated about a flaming cauldron and chant The Goddess Chant, but typically, our love for The Charges of the Goddess moves us to include this moving, powerful dialogue between Priestess and Universe, between Goddess and those who hear Her words. I do not wish to enter the controversy over the origins of these words other than to say that whomever wrote them ought be considered divinely inspired and worthy of our perpetual gratitude. I know of no other sacred literature which has brought such a unity of beliefs and of imagery to the Wiccan

world of the twentieth century. This text is as it was passed
me, and comes from the Traditional sources of modern neo-
paganism, many of which are but decades old.

The Priestess stands before the Priest. His hands rest gently
upon her shoulders and her arms are crossed before her, in the
position of a body which has been laid to rest. As the Priestess
drops into a deep, trance-like state in which she brings together
all her training to set aside her ego, the Priest prepares the
temple with these words:

> Listen to the words of the Great Mother: She, Who was of
> old also called among mortals, Artemis, Astarte, Athene;
> Dione, Melusine, Aphrodite; Cerridwen, Dana Arionrhod;
> Isis, Bride, and by many other Names:

And from the Priestess arises some of the most beautiful
poetry the world has ever heard:

> Whenever ye have need of anything, once in the month and
> better it be when the Moon is Full, then shall ye assemble in
> some secret place and adore the Spirit of Me, Who am
> Queen of all the Witches.
>
> There shall ye assemble, ye who are fain to learn all
> sorcery yet have not won its deepest secrets; to these will I
> teach things that are as yet unknown. And ye shall be free
> from slavery, and as a token that ye be really free, ye shall be
> naked in your rites and ye shall dance, sing, feast, make
> music and love all in My praise. For Mine is the ecstasy of
> the Spirit and Mine also is joy upon Earth, for My love is
> law unto all beings.
>
> Keep pure your Highest Ideals; strive ever toward
> them, let naught stop you nor turn you aside, for Mine is
> the secret door which opens upon the door of youth. And
> Mine is the Cup of the Wine of Life and the Cauldron of
> Cerridwen, which is the Holy Grail of Immortality.
>
> I am the Gracious Goddess, Who gives the gift of joy
> unto the hearts of men and women. Upon Earth I give
> knowledge of the Spirit Eternal and beyond death I give

peace, freedom and reunion with those who have gone before. Nor do I demand sacrifice, for behold, I am the Mother of all living and My love is poured out upon the Earth.

They pause. Their Magick permeates the Temple. In the right combination of stage presence and strict mental discipline, a Priestess can truly become transformed in this process. Yet, although these have been the words of the Goddess, who is She? Who is this Divine Woman? The second of the two Charges is that primary work of modern Wiccan literature which explains, conceptually, what is meant when we say the Goddess. The Priest introduces the second of the Charges. As he does so, She awakens. Having now risen from the Underworld, for these Charges are a version of the Legend of the Goddess' Descent Into Death and Rebirth, her arms unfold and her fingers reach out to the corners of the universe. The Priest's hands follow hers, providing physical support and a balance of energy as the Priestess stands in the star position, which might be considered a Wiccan asana.

Hear ye the words of the Star Goddess, She in the dust of Whose feet are the hosts of heaven, Whose body encircles the Universe . . .

And the Priestess responds, in the most beautiful words I have ever heard:

I am the beauty of the green Earth, and the white Moon among the stars, and the Mysteries of the waters, and the desire in the hearts of humans.

Call unto thy soul, arise and come unto Me, for I am the Soul of Nature, Who gives life to the Universe. From Me all things proceed and unto Me all things must return. And before My face, beloved of Gods and of humans, let thine innermost divine self be enfolded in the rapture of the Infinite.

Let My worship be within the heart that rejoiceth, for

behold, all acts of love and pleasure are My rituals, therefore let there be beauty and strength, power and compassion, honor and humility, mirth and reverence with you. And thou, who thinkest to seek for Me, know that the seeking and yearning shall avail thee not unless thou knowest the Mystery: that if that which thou seekest, thou findest not within thee, thou shalt never find it without thee. For behold, I have been with thee from the beginning and I am that which is attained at the end of desire.

Invoking the God

In the Tradition of Lothlorien, we invoke that aspect of the God called the Poetryman, for as an archetype, He would be considered very conservative of our natural resources and highly concerned about the care given our fellow humans. But let Him speak for Himself. The Priest stands and draws the energy of the God-as-Archetype through his crystal ball as he turns and intones the words of The Charge of Lothlorien:

Then you shall be taught to be wise, so in the fullness of time you shall count yourselves among those who serve the Ancients; And you shall grow to love the music of the Woodlands, to dance to the sound of His pipes in step with cloven hooves and the forest song . . .

And you shall learn the Mystery of Rebirth, filling your heart with Her moonlight, growing in harmony with the Earth, as Her children, protective of your Mother . . .

And you shall grow in wisdom; and you shall grow in compassion. And in love shall you heal the sick, pursuing the arts of healing, the lore of the Mother's herbes . . . learning the psychic arts . . . to cure, to nurture, to help Her children grow. And in wisdom you shall give counsel, knowing the skills of divination, seeing how the children best flow in Universal Harmony, understanding planetary cycles and knowing prophecy.

Thus will you be the Wise Ones, knowing the lores of

Nature; the Wiccans of the heaths, of the countryside, the pagans of the cities, knowing all are One to the Mother; knowing all are One to the Father.

Let thy life and the lives to come be in the service of the Lord and the Lady.

Raising a Cone of Power

Now have we brought to this space all of the energies we shall wish to bring together in this one act of Magick. Each step thus far is like a single ingredient within a complex and stunning recipe. There is no greater ritual tool than the self. The culmination of the ritual work we have done thus far is now brought together through the use of the self as a ritual tool to mix these energies. The concept of a small group of people, holding hands and dancing in a Circle, rhythmically, each moving in simultaneous step to create some figurative cone, is generally very confusing to the Novice.

Consider that Wiccans believe all power comes from the self. Then we might see a Circle of individual powers, now yoking themselves together, chanting the same chant in unison, visualizing an assortment of symbols in unison, and each functioning as focused, intensified auric energy, the threads of which flow behind the dancer. As all move together, it is as if a large magneto is functioning and the bright-coloured threads of the glowing auras become bound in a woven fabric of thought forms which is likened to a cone. But there is no explanation I could provide to communicate that which must be felt in person. All I can say is that it is real. The energy created through dancing and chanting The Witches' Rune is palpable and glorious, overwhelming and inspiring. The rhythm begins slow and careful, the volume measured. Slowly the tempo is increased, the chanting intensified but as the final verse is repeated, rather than increasing in volume, the energy is controlled and focused through a decrescendo. The effect is very, very potent.

This introduces the second of those passages of which the

30

source may be considered unknown, but which modern
pagan texts tend to overlay with many romantic attributions.
This chant is perhaps the second most popular work of
unifying literature, and although I have seen a variety of
versions, this is the way it was passed on to me. There is often
much dispute over some of the meanings. The phrase Queen
of Hell, for example, can have a multitude of interpretations
and the true meanings of the final words are far too many to be
relevant. We have our own interpretation of their meaning, but
as you repeat the final verse three times, you must learn for
yourself.

> Darksome night and shining Moon
> East then South then West then North,
> Hearken to the Witches' Rune
> Here I come to call thee forth!
>
> Earth and water, air and fire,
> Wand and pentacle and sword:
> Work ye unto my desire,
> Hearken ye unto my word!
>
> Cords and censer, scourge and knife,
> Powers of the Witch's blade:
> Waken all ye unto life,
> Come ye as the charm is made!
>
> Queen of Heaven, Queen of Hell!
> Horned Hunter of the night,
> Lend your power unto my spell
> And work my will by magick rite;
>
> By all the power of land and sea,
> By all the might of Moon and Sun
> As I do will so Mote It Be:
> Chant the spell and be it done!
>
> Eko, Eko, Azarak!
> Eko, Eko, Zamilak!

Eko, Eko, Karnayna!
Eko, Eko, Aradia!

Everything stops suddenly and there are only the sounds of breathing as the participants use breath control, visualization and mental disciplines to channel as much power as possible through the image or item which is the primary focus of the ritual's performance. There may be times when we do this work to bless seeds for the garden, or send the power to an individual who desires to enact self-healing. The intensity of the temple at this time is palpable, and when the energy begins to settle down, there is nothing else one can do but have a simple celebration, for now we have moved beyond words.

Cakes and Wine

We celebrate what we have done by sharing some manner of bread or cake made by one of our members. We also share wine, which is usually an herbal, non-alcoholic drink. These are blessed and passed around the Circle. It is the physical bonding of unity which works as the counterpart to the magickal, psychic bonding which took place during the Cone of Power. This also provides us with an opportunity to relax our disciplines and concentrations and to visit lightly, although it must be remembered that this Circle remains primed, ready to take all thought and deed and empower them. The sharing of cakes and wine is but a pause for reflection.

Closing the Circle

It is inevitable that the closing of the Circle seem anti-climactic, for that is its very nature. Yet there must be completion and balance to the sacred proceedings. The work is now complete, and the components of a Circle, as with any tool, must now be placed in safekeeping.

The energies of the four quarters are first addressed. Because an action was initiated to bring forth these archetypes, a closure must be effected. The Priest/ess takes up the athame and in the East scribes a Banishing Air Pentagram which, in effect, erases the invocation of that Watchtower. S/he extinguishes the candle and tends to the physical items which comprise the Eastern altar. Then, raising his/her athame s/he says:

> Lords of the East
> Creatures of Air

Banishing Air Pentagram

> We thank you this night
> For all blessings fair.

Everyone present uses these words to give thanks to all symbols and associations of this quarter and to release any of the energy which may remain, unused in the generation of the Cone of Power. In addition, all visualizations which have been established must be released. The Priest/ess then goes to the South:

> Lords of the South
> Creatures of Fire

Banishing Fire Pentagram

We thank you for showing us
Growth and desire.

As this process of release is performed, other actions, such as the extinguishing of the candles in each of the four directions may be accomplished. Walking to the West, the form continues:

Lords of the West
Creatures of Water

Banishing Water Pentagram

We thank you for bringing
Eternity's daughter.

And in the North:

Lords of the North,
Gods of the trees,

Banishing Earth Pentagram

We join in your worship
Of Earth harmonies.

In the Tradition of Lothlorien, any performance of the Great Rite, that Sacred Union in which two individuals will come together romantically and/or sexually, representing a conjunction of the Divine Polarities, is believed best done in private. This is out of respect for individuals, as we place no limitations nor restrictions upon that form of ritual work. In the Ritual of Lothlorien, however, the Great Rite is performed symbolically. It is for this reason that it enters the Ritual only when The Work has already entered its declination, for the Great Rite will be performed in private, later, following the completion of the ritual.

The Great Rite may later be performed between the working couple, or between any two (or more) persons, whether they have both attended or not. It is not uncommon for those who have attended to later turn to their homes to join their partners-in-sensuality.

For the Great Rite, as performed symbolically, the Priest kneels before the Priestess and takes the special chalice in his hands. He holds it for her as she takes her athame and slowly lowers it into the chalice and says:

> In the union of polarities, in the Perfect Balance, do we create and sing in joy of Perfect Love. In the sharing of this cup may we all know that the coming together of God and Goddess, of Moon and Sun, of Love and Trust, brings forth the birth, the True Creation. So Mote It Be!

The cup is passed deosil and all commune through sharing a taste of the sacred herbal drink or wine, as the case may be. When it returns, the Priestess drinks the final draught and sets it upon the altar, saying,

> May we all share our love and Magick in all the Circles of Time. We leave for now this Rite and close this Circle. This Rite ends in joy.

And here follows one of our best traditions: everyone present hugs everyone else.

Chapter III
Learning to Step with Care: The Nature of Pathworking

Among the greatest of challenges facing modern Wicca lies in the education of those who will carry our religion and our Traditions into the future. The survival of any religious sect or Tradition is dependant upon members who are capable of perpetuating it with respect for the established forms and written religious materials, yet allowing for continued evolution and creativity. An established Mystery Tradition provides a path, one followed from a would-be Novice's first interest until the passing into the Bardo state between lives. A path is worked by a student, with guidance from a Mentor or teacher.

What is pathworking? In its simplest definition, it would be the process of doing the work which enables one to follow a path. The word is applicable to any form of path, whether it be a martial art or spiritual discipline. An objective view of pathworking might compare it with many other studies such as musical and artistic disciplines, which require practise and guidance from a teacher, or even career paths which involve commitment and diligence, among other attributes.

To work a chosen, spiritually disciplined path one must be capable of taking sure steps, of having adequate guidance as to the options one has regarding routing and safe passage into the unknown. As with any journey, a map is most helpful in attaining a goal.

A newcomer to any path frequently has a rose-hazed vision of the path's ultimate end. Enthusiastic idealism has not yet been tempered. Waiting for such a student, the future holds challenges, changes and the pain encountered when one experiences growth. The onset of harsh reality may bring devastating consequences to a student's pathworking commitment. For those who guide students, one of the earliest aspects of training is the responsibility of providing adequate knowledge of difficulties likely to be encountered and of realistic descriptions of the end results for those who do complete the journey.

It is very important that a new student who has requested training be given a reasonable understanding of what lies in store. What lies in store means much more than curriculum. The embracing of a religious lifestyle, of a specific, traditional way of expressing those beliefs (even in an eclectic, non-structured Tradition) holds changes which will affect one's lifestyle and future direction. A new student ought have a reasonable understanding of all aspects of the path. The nature of a mystery religion is such that it is impossible to provide as full an understanding of a path as would be desirable, but a reasonable goal is to present the student with adequate information for the first stages of growth. Then, having gleaned familiarity with the nature of that path, the student will be able to ascertain whether or not to remain with this particular system of spirituality. One cannot expect to successfully complete any portion of a path unless one brings a sense of commitment towards completion of certain goals and an understanding of what lies ahead.

The process of teaching the Mysteries is a far greater challenge than that of just being a Witch. Caretaking is a strong tendency for many of us, yet Mother Nature is willing to push a bird from the nest to teach it the skill of flight. We must be willing to test students, to make them demonstrate a well-grounded desire to pursue study with a serious intent. We should demand no less of our students than do the teachers of mainstream religion.

Wiccan paths often hold a strong interest for people interested in spiritual development. In a great number of Traditions, Initiation is granted only upon the completion of a variety of studies, preparatory training and the acquisition of skills. These differences are often a primary aspect which distinguishes one Tradition from another. Some Traditions of Wicca initiate a person prior to any training. At the other end of the scale are Traditions which require very extensive training. The Tradition of Lothlorien is among the latter. Working with a large community of members, it is felt that training should be comparable to the ministerial training of other religions. In presenting the training system of The Mystery School, it is done so in order to provide ideas with which you might better examine your own considerations.

Any path should see as its goal the training of teachers capable of continuing that Tradition in such a fashion that it survives, reasonably intact. This must be done in such a manner that the freedom to continue the process of creation be balanced with a respect for that Tradition which has already been created. It is also important to consider the nature of the community which is currently being served and also the future potential of that community. Without those who are learning, we are nothing.

The First Steps of the Path

In the Tradition of Lothlorien, those who guide others along our Path include not only the College of Mentors (which comprise the faculty) but also those who are undergoing their teacher-training (Priest/esses who are First Degree Initiates) and now and then a Novice who needs such an assignment to further her/his studies. We make a careful distinction between the teaching of a Mystery Tradition, which can only be done when one has knowledge, and the teaching of other lore and knowledge, in which all are teachers.

What are the goals of the College of Mentors? Through preparing students for initiation on a one-to-one basis, care is given to instill the concept of a Higher Priest/esshood in Novices. This implies a Priest/esshood which transcends denominational preference. We believe that there is kinship among all who share in The Work. The Work is a phrase which encompasses the bringing of religious truths and spiritual awareness; of teaching the great, nondenominational Mysteries of love for this planet as a manifestation of Divinity. The Work is done throughout all Ages and among all cultures. The Higher Priest/esshood includes persons in numerous religions who are all working to keep the Mysteries alive in numerous ways to reach as many people as possible regardless of personal beliefs.

We encourage students to pursue their Highest Ideals and to integrate an ever-increasing ethical nature into daily living. It is important that one not merely study the Craft, but develop the ability to live as a Priest/ess at all times. Because a student's needs, skills and goals are equally important, a written application is required. This provides a Mentor with a better understanding of the student's background, both strengths and weaknesses, and establishes a dialogue in which a student learns to become comfortable in discussing her or his own abilities in a non-judgemental manner. The application form states that a student agrees to accept the form of training The Mystery School provides and that this will be for a twelve month period. Contractual agreement is a very interesting concept for the Craft. One of the maxims of the modern Craft is that a Witch is only as good as her/his word. The process of writing a contract for a year's study causes the student to think more seriously about the nature of that commitment. Not only is the twelve-month agreement the initial stage of the student's entry into The Mystery School, but continuing students reapply on an annual basis. Reapplication causes deep thought about the seriousness of study. We have seen a considerable number of students recognize major questions lurking beneath the surface of consciousness which might otherwise have gone unfound. Reapplication also causes the student to make a careful reflection of the nature of the previous year's progress and challenges. As my teacher once impressed upon me the importance of making a student ask for knowledge, sometimes more than once, The Mystery School has a would-be student ask, in writing, to become a Novice. Students who have learned to ask, listen far more carefully. Upon admission to our training, they are then considered Novice Supplicants, or those who have requested admission to the Novitiate. These are students who have agreed to accept the ideas put forth in The Admonition. The introduction of ethics in the teaching of a religious lifestyle must be one of the priorities of any training. When students enter The Mystery School, they are admonished to begin deep consideration, to establish habits of careful thought regarding the Pathworking before them. This is the first Sacred Key (Book of Shadows material written for the Tradition of Lothlorien — a key for unlocking internal Mysteries) which the new student receives. It is important to create your Tradition so that it speaks for itself. The Admonition has remained nearly verbatim since first written in 1977, following a state of inspiration which followed the initiations of two Canadian Priestesses. It is a fortunate teacher to have students who bring inspiration.

Those of us who have spent years in this Tradition have found that no amount of time nor training have diminished the meaning of these words. The Admonition opens with a puzzle. Immediately, with the next lesson to transcribe for the Book of Shadows, the student will also receive a reading list. This is not the only enigma within this desideratum, for one of its goals is to stimulate thought and provoke discussion. But now let The Admonition speak for itself:

> One does not read about the Wicca.
> One does not study about the Craft of the Wise.
> The knowledge I will teach is not idle:
> You can only learn this knowledge if you use it — if you put it to work.
> This study is only for those who have a willingness to learn.
> Each of you has expressed a desire to learn.
> Each of you has shown talent at being magickal — at making things happen.
> If you are to learn the Craft, you must swear that you will work all your Magick in Perfect Love.

Work negative magick and you are not one of us.

You must work at growing positive, even if it requires change.

Each of you has shown that you are capable of making changes in the self, in order that your Magick be more positive.

Each of you has learned that change allows you to be happier.

To learn the Craft of Wicca, you must make changes.

Each of you has done this, and it is joyous and beautiful of you, and it is this happiness we share.

At this level of your training, you must maintain secrecy.

If your friends, your family, your lovers were truly ready for this knowledge, they would be here — now.

But if they are not; that is proof that they are not yet ready.

Speak no Magick to those who know less than you, unless you are prepared to tell all of us that you are a teacher of the Craft.

A true teacher does not teach the Craft until s/he has completed the training.

If those we are with are in positive Craft Traditions, we can speak to our peers and to those more wise than ourselves.

Each of you has your own timing.

You learn at your own rate.

Should you leave this study, there is no sorrow, only joy at the love we have shared.

Each of you has shown the ability to work together to raise good, positive energy.

Each of you knows how to help and to share.

Each of you will learn to trust each other.

You must have with me Perfect Trust.

If you do not trust me as your Mentor, I cannot teach you.

And I give you Perfect Trust.

If you swear to trust me, it is because I swear that I trust you.

You have not arrived here by chance.

You have displayed a desire to learn.

You have displayed a talent at Magick.

This Magick is to heal, to help; it only works in Perfect Love.

You are here because you have shown us that you are learning to work in Perfect Love.

It is the only way to happiness; and you are here because you are growing in happiness.

You are learning to unlock joy.

Each of you is capable of becoming a teacher — to learn the Craft of Wicca and to share that knowledge.

Each of you must grow into becoming a teacher.

Each of you has taken the Path of being willing to learn, the Path of wanting to learn.

Each of you is growing.

Each of you is creative.

Each of you is special to the Magick of the Universe.

Each of you perceives the Magick of the Universe as a balance of Yin and Yang,

of masculine and feminine,

of God and Goddess.

Each of you recognizes the feminine and masculine within the self.

Each of you has been told this knowledge is only for those who seek to become of the Wicca.

Each of you is here because it is felt by the Wise, by the Wicca, that you are capable of knowing stronger Magick than you have thus far conceived of.

By being here, now, you have demonstrated a desire to take this Path.

You have already begun.

You are here because you have shown love to the World.

Because you, also, are Wise.

The Wicca means the Wise: The Wise Ones.

We meet together to talk as wise people and celebrate our happiness.

All of us, even your teachers, are pursuing wisdom and we all follow the Laws.

To complete this study, to follow this Path into Initiation means you will be ready to celebrate the Wisdom you have attained, to celebrate in ritual the knowledge that you are Magick;

To share with us wine and happiness, words of beauty and laughter . . .

By the time you complete this course of study you will be a Priest/ess of Lothlorien and an Initiated Child of the God and the Goddess.

Dedicating Oneself to a Path

It is not possible to teach ethics without some introduction of those dreams which enable a student to perceive future reality. Within the study of astrology, Sagittarius is that zodiacal sign which most prefers intellectual pursuit and challenge. Inherent in the Sage, (a manifestation of Sagittarius), is the mixture of realistic knowledge combined with dreams for an improved, enlightened future. The teaching of religion is no different. The very nature of many belief systems is found in their dream-relationships with an enlightened future, escape from the present into a future haven or in a future which enables the follower to move into a state of being which is most assuredly an improvement over the present. The manner in which religions keep those dreams alive directly affects astral realities and the manner of lifestyle within the guidelines of that religion determines the Bardo realm to be encountered at death. Wicca is like other religions. There are certain goals which are common to most Traditions, such as those of reincarnation and others which are found, for example, within The Charges of the Goddess. In addition there are those

44

Wiccan goals which vary from Tradition to Tradition. These goals should be presented to the student as soon as is feasible. Because many of the goals in our religions involve guiding a student into and through various Mysteries, this process requires varying levels of commitment from the student. In the Tradition of Lothlorien this is accomplished both through the student's written application and contractual agreement for study in yearly increments and by becoming Dedicated, through ritual, as a Novice. This is not an initiatory process by any means but serves as a ceremonial celebration of a student's personal covenant to her/his own study. It is a process through which a mature decision is ritually blessed in order to confirm one's faith in the Path which lies ahead.

Although not an initiatory ritual, change is inherent in the Ritual of Dedication. Numerically, this might be thought of as the nature of change in the number two. There is a before and an after, but it is not as complex as are the evolutionary processes implied in the other numerical values of change. The First Degree Initiation, for example, would be that of the number three, which implies transformation at its simplest level. Second Degree Initiation is a similar transformation, but one which can only attain completion while maintaining responsibilities at the same time, a far more difficult matter and that of a numerical value of five. But Dedication is a simple declaration, one which which deserves a ritual of beauty.

Supplicants become Novices by ritually dedicating themselves to the Tradition of Lothlorien. As the student agrees to dedicate time, effort and resources to the pursuit of this study, in turn does the Priest/ess dedicate blessings to the student. The Candidate for Dedication arrives, having prepared both physically and spiritually for the occasion. The ritual form is kept simple, generic, and often non-verbal until the question is posed:

> Do you wish to be Dedicated to the Lady of the Moon, who spills Her love into the night; do you wish to be Dedicated to the Lord of the Sun Who shines in glory upon Her

fields? Do you seek to learn of the cycles and the ways in which we share in them? Do you desire to learn of the Craft of Wicca and to learn to gaze upon your inner Mysteries?

Because this ritual is very personal for a new Novice, the Priest/ess remains behind the student and everything which is said aloud is treated as if the dialogue of this ritual is between the student and the Universe. The Priest/ess functions as the artistic medium through which the poetic imagery flows. As the student responds in the affirmative, the Priest/ess begins to read the blessings:

'May the Lord and Lady give you visions of joy. May They fill your rituals with songs of love and creation . . .

'May the Goddess and God sing you songs of wisdom and may your heart be filled with Divine music . . .

'May your songs fill the night and your love pour out as the laughing of a stream . . .

'May your chants be butterflies in the breeze, the cry of the lone bird, the might of thunder, the sigh of a new-born baby . . .

'May you fill your rituals with songs to praise the Mother, to honor the Father . . .

'May you love Them Both as One. You have come here to share in Them, to grow of Their wisdom. You seek to follow Their Paths.'

A number of the beliefs of Wiccan Traditions are found in the next passages which the Priest/ess reads for the Novice Supplicant:

'You have not arrived here by chance. You have put yourself on this Path long ago. We shall walk some of it together and rejoice. We first began in past sorrows, in past lives. We were of the Wicca, gazing at the stars, feeling deep unnamed secrets; touching the Earth in joy and sensing life within; seeing birth and knowing that it was a miracle, a

Mystery, a joy; being still in the forest, being warm in the water . . .

'We are all lights, and we follow the Path through the God and the Goddess, by all Their names, and in growing, we grow in brightness, following the cycles of Sun and Moon, and glowing in Divine Radiance.'

Lest these beliefs get lost behind the poetry, they should be presented clearly. The concept of reincarnation, of the human desire to uplift the soul and elevate it towards Divine perfection is very strong in modern Wicca. But there are also past sorrows which arise out of our present incarnation, those which trap us before we learn to accept responsibility for the directions and events of our lives and before we have learned to change those things we find intolerable. We must accept that which we cannot change. We must learn to find pleasure in those things we would not wish to change. We must change those things about ourselves which displease us but we have no right to change others unless they have requested it of us. And if we cannot change something and it causes us displeasure, then we must go inside and change our attitudes. So many of those attracted to Wicca spent their childhoods with greater difficulties, for so many of us had stronger intuitions, precognitive dreams, or other manifestations which are more romantic than practical but which in past eras were the mark of the village healer, the shaman, priestess or witch doctor. So many of us were, just simply, more intense than our classmates. So many of us had perceptions of reality or even perceptions of our selves and our sensualities which did not fit in a structured world which believes that pantheism is inherently evil and sex, while not necessarily evil, is of questionable good unless one shares in the overpopulation of an already-strained planet.

We are those who do gaze at the stars, both for the manner in which they move our souls and inspire us to attain greater perfection in our lives and for the insights we gain from observing their patterns. For most Wiccans, astrology remains an essential tool of the Priest/esshood. This has been true for thousands of years and remains so today. Everything is Divine: God is everywhere. If God/dess is in the stars, then surely an understanding of their patterns will be of use to my life, for God/dess is there, also.

In like manner do we take joy in our Earth, exploring the forests, the rivers, the rainbows and the raging forest fire alike. Nature provides, for the Witch, the clearest path to understanding those conventions which are necessary for civilization. Nature may be beautiful, but it is neither good nor evil. Nature is a more direct manifestation of the Divine than is the human. It is for that reason that the sexual aspect of nature, which brings together male and female for reproduction and is also sexual apart from reproduction, sets our deifications of the Universe quite apart from those of the Judeo-Christian religions. We have more in common with the Buddhists of the Tibetan tantric ritual known as the Bardo Thodol in which the deity personifies both male and female and is often translated as a Father-Mother.

Curriculum

There are many challenges which face a Mentor. One must do more than provide intellectual fodder. A good teacher imparts wisdom, but not only the wisdom of a teacher which might help light the path as does the lantern of the Hermit's lamp in the tarot. True wisdom is unfolded from within, as a lotus. A Mentor must instruct a student in the value of discipline, providing adequate challenges and allowing a student to learn from trial and error. The responsibility of learning to embrace discipline as a work of love ought be shared by Mentor and student alike.

In the preparation of clergy, regardless of denomination, there are many skills required which cannot be learned from textbooks. Attributes of ministry must be understood. A conscious being must be given the tools which provide an expanded awareness of the more subtle aspects of ministry and healing. In THE TRAINING AND WORK OF AN INITIATE,

Dion Fortune writes,

> 'the good occult student should have a sound general
> knowledge of natural science, history, mathematics and
> philosophy. He cannot, naturally, have a thorough
> knowledge of all these subjects, but he should know their
> outlines; he should be familiar with the principles of all the
> sciences and know the methods of philosophy. Then, when
> he acquires special knowledge, he will be able to see it in
> relation to the cosmic scheme of which it forms a part, and
> hence will know it in a very different way from the man who
> perceives it apart from its environment.'

In The Mystery School of the Rowan Tree, training not only
prepares a student, through one-on-one guidance, for
initiation, but care is given to instill in the Novice a concept of a
Higher Priest/esshood. I deeply believe in the Higher Priest/
esshood. I have encountered some of those who share that
belief, both in this incarnate reality and in astral realities. It is a
Priest/esshood which transcends denominational difference.
These teachers incarnate in ways which enable them to best
accomplish their work in a certain period of historical
evolution. Your individual evolution as a soul may well dictate
that you spend some of your incarnations in mainstream
religions in addition to your chosen, Earth-oriented path. The
further one progresses along the development of Priest/
esshood, the more one should be able to see the basic truths
which, to some degree or another, permeate all religions.

In addition, a student must learn to become better
integrated into cultural reality. By this is meant an increasing
sense of union with one's neighborhood, one's political and
social environment. Ministry and healing are more effective
when we work to remove those barriers which separate us from
others in our society. Although I live within the framework of a
highly alternative religion, my Wiccan training has allowed me
to develop an awareness and gather knowledge which has
enabled me to freely and joyfully discuss religion with many,

laypersons & clergy alike, who, if they knew I was a Witch, would probably react with shock, quickly erecting barriers to any further communication.

The curriculum is given a brief outline in The Charge of Lothlorien . . .

> 'Then you shall be taught to be wise, so in the fullness of time you shall count yourself among those who serve the Ancient Ones;
>
> 'And you shall grow to love the music of the Woodlands, to dance to the sound of His pipes, in step with cloven hooves and the forest song;
>
> 'And you shall learn the Mystery of rebirth, filling your heart with Her moonlight, growing in harmony with the Earth, as Her child, protective of your Mother;
>
> 'And you shall grow in wisdom.
>
> 'And you shall grow in compassion.
>
> 'And in love shall you heal the sick, pursuing the arts of healing, the lore of the Mother's herbes, learning the psychic arts to cure, to nurture, to help Her children grow . . .
>
> 'And in wisdom you shall give counsel, knowing the skills of divination, seeing how the children best flow in Universal Harmony; understanding planetary cycles and knowing prophecy . . .
>
> 'Thus will you be of the Wise Ones, knowing the lores of Nature, the Wiccans of the heaths, of the countryside, the pagans of the cities . . . Knowing all are one to the Mother, knowing all are one to the Father.'

Among these lovely lines is an introduction to the ministry of Lothlorien. Required are the attributes of wisdom and compassion, plus the ability to take joy at the music of Nature, the freedom of soul which enables one's feet to dance at a ritual. It takes skill to fill your heart with moonlight. Far more than an emotional swoon, there are serious ritual disciplines which await a student, bringing skills which create spiritual unity with the Moon's powers.

A minister is to be trained in healing skills, including herbals, spiritual healing and other forms. The development of psychic skills is not done for personal gain but to enhance The Work. A minister is trained in counselling skills. A minister of the Mysteries is also trained to move into the Divine, whether through the cards of tarot or through dreams, to utilize intuition in seeking answers which might alleviate another's troubles. In addition, astrological knowledge is necessary for the observation of patterns so that one can counsel others in learning to flow with change and avoid undue stress.

With these goals in mind, the Novice Supplicant requests the blessings of the Ritual and is dedicated to the attainment of the Higher Priest/esshood through the Path of Lothlorien:

'Let thy life and the lives to come be in the service of the Lord and Lady.'

The Mystery School Curriculum

The first level of study for a new student involves reading a series of introductory essays. These welcome the student to the pathworking and begin providing some background information on the history and nature of our training system. This provides the means of introducing vocabulary so that students and Mentors will share a common language. It also provides a student with written expectations, procedures and methods of introducing the Mysteries, even as many schools provide a handbook of miscellaneous information.

Other essays describe the manner in which we approach our Books of Shadows and establish procedures: for adding additional portions of the written Tradition, regularly meeting with a Mentor to mutually evaluate progress and seek solutions for difficulties. They cover a variety of views of the nature of ministry which help a student better understand whether or not that is a path to which s/he wishes to make a commitment, for this should be done prior to any ritualized taking of vows, even at a non-initiatory level such as Dedication.

Upon the completion of the first essay, a student is asked to self-determine an adequate level of comprehension. The student then requests, in writing, the next essay. There are certain values in this approach. Self-evaluation must be developed as a constant office of ministry, particularly when one's life grows increasingly bound by magickal skill, for a path which takes one ever further into Magick is one which increases the power of the individual, whether positive or negative. A state of Magickal Being is ever-present amd Magick is inherently neither good nor evil.

Magick is the process of creation. By embracing Magickal Being, all which one creates becomes increasingly empowered, whether a carefully constructed ritual of healing or a casual, angry emotion flung at another person. It is the obligatory function of a Priest/ess to sustain an ever-present conscience which observes and judges all action and thought with standards ever-raised as the path is progressed.

This written approach to the essays also gives the student several responsibilities. It is written in The Admonition that each of us has our own timing. It becomes the student's own determination which illustrates to the Mentor the rate of progress in effect as the student begins pathworking. Further, established from the very beginning are the early levels of communication skills. Students learn that they must ask, directly, for more study material. Too often do students assume that spiritual teachers have uncanny gifts and psychic skills enabling them to know just where the student is along the path, automatically increasing or decreasing the rate of training. Good teaching involves dialogue between the Mentor and the student.

When the essays have been read, a simple course of study is presented to the student to complete prior to Dedication. This involves study of The Admonition and of The Ritual of Dedic-ation, a basic ritual form which is used in the Dedication, and the beginnings of research and analysis. The first books of the reading list are encountered, providing a student with a good Wiccan sourcebook of generic rituals for a variety of occasions, in addition to a view of Wicca which differs from that of Lothlorien (A BOOK OF PAGAN RITUALS). A strong foundation in the similarities and differences among many Wiccan Traditions is essential. A more intimate view of our own Tradition is provided in THE HOLY BOOKS OF THE DEVAS.

Required, also, is an excellent book which provides a fascinating view of one woman's journey. Alexandra David-Neel, a highly controversial figure, studied at a number of mystery schools in Tibet recording her observations in the early twentieth century, long before Tibet was accessible to Western travelers. MAGIC AND MYSTERY IN TIBET also provides engaging anecdotes showing the lengths to which serious students went and the hardships endured in order to achieve the skills of an adept. Although this book is written about Tibet when that Land of Snows was still secluded from modern realities, preserving its ancient, pre-industrialized culture, the text gives a modern student additional role models. As one student wrote, the book opened up for me many ideas and practises I had not thought of. It expanded my understanding of psychic phenomena and disciplines as well as methods of study and the number of years involved.

The first Quest is encountered. A Quest is a process by which a student is given a task to complete and must develop individual resourcefulness to achieve the goal. Quests carry a bit of romantic nostalgia and memories of Arthurian legends, but they are also valuable teaching aids. A Quest is only valid when both Mentor and student are in agreement. It provides a student the opportunity to begin learning the value of keeping one's word, and of the intricacies in giving one's word regarding the accomplishment of tasks.

In this first Quest, the student is instructed to choose a candle of the appropriate colour. Such a seemingly ambiguous phrase is indicative of pathworking in a mystery tradition. One student will carefully study a number of books from the library, covering topics on candles, on colours and upon simple magick. Another student will intuitively request to use a certain colour, based solely upon an internal feeling. Neither approach is better. The task of choosing one's candle for Dedication and of completing written answers for study guides begins to open the first petals of the student's inner lotus as one embarks upon the Path of Lothlorien.

Following Dedication, the curriculum is sometimes compared, albeit loosely, to a bachelor's degree, during which the student assembles the skills, tools and knowledge necessary to begin practising as a Priest/ess in solitary fashion. There are two levels of work prior to the first Initiation. Each level of work is called an Ordeal, although it is the student (and not the Path) who tends to make the work an ordeal. When the student completes the list of tasks to do, books to read, things to copy and things to write s/he must undergo oral exams. In the testing of a student, it is important that the student not be judged as passing or failing: inadequate knowledge is also the result of a Mentor's oversight.

There is a substantial amount of written Tradition to transcribe into one's own Book of Shadows. The manner in which Lothlorien assigns magickal symbols, colors, elemental creatures, etc. is included in a set of four Keys, each of which opens the door to an understanding of the four elements and directions. The student is given the text of our primary ritual form, The Ritual of Lothlorien as it exists in our Book of Shadows. In addition, the student spends extensive time studying The Charges of The Goddess and The Witch's Rune, both of which are not only common to most Traditions (with slight variation) but which contain the very essence of Wiccan ideology.

The primary tools which a Novice assembles include an athame, with a traditional ritual of consecration based upon Lothlorien's Wiccan and Alexandrian heritage, and a chalice.

Secondary tools include brand new written material, for the beginning the student brings forth personal crea..vity, writing materials on the four elements and other topics. This is very useful both for students who remain with the Tradition of Lothlorien and also for many who have studied for several years and then gone on to create their own Traditions.

The work of a Novice includes learning to keep a journal and learning several forms of introspection. One exercise in contemplation includes a series of questions. In sharing these with you, I would like to express gratitude to Artemis, who was a Priestess with Lothlorien for several years before moving into her Buddhist Tradition. She wrote the major portions of these guidelines.

1. Examine your feelings regarding structured Path working. Is structure useful?
2. How do the shared 'format' and limitations set by Pathworking promote individual freedom and growth?
3. What is spiritual authority? How is it bestowed upon humans? What is the ideal distribution of authority between Mentor and Novice?
4. Examine the hierarchical structure of The Mystery School. Examine hierarchical structure within mystery traditions and as a general religious phenomenon.
5. Make a list of the adjectives you use in perceiving your magickal self. Why do you use them? How are they applicable?
6. Why is this Path compatible with your Highest Ideals? what purpose does it serve?
7. Is 'religious truth; relative or absolute?
8. Contemplate your attitudes toward mainstream religions; toward your childhood religion; and toward new religions. Reconcile any negative emotions.
9. What is the primary source and purpose of evil? How do you protect yourself against it?
10. Contemplate self-healing. How have you used your studies to promote the psychic healing of inner-wounds?

11. Contemplate methods of evoking internal and external changes. How are they connected? What is cyclical change? Linear change? Initiatory change?

12. Contemplate your personal attitudes toward masculinity and femininity as they exist internally within yourself and externally within social culture.

13. Analyze your attitudes toward secrecy. How does secrecy relate to the ideals of openness and honesty? Is it possible to manifest strength and to progress in silence?

In learning the art of ritual performance, not only does the Novice spend time both studying and later learning to perform the Ritual of Lothlorien, but is also directed to research one of the several variations of The Lesser Banishing Pentagram Ritual, easily found among the many texts on Magick. Providing additional background on this ritual form, which we use as an exercise much as an aspiring concert pianist learns etudes, is the text THE MIDDLE PILLAR.

To be considered ready for the first Initiation, one must be capable of performing ritual with reasonable skill and of understanding the natures of both formal ritual work and of extemporaneous work. Our First Degree of Initiation empowers a Priest/ess. Even before this power is conferred, a Novice must begin community service to explore the personal validity of such a vocation. Being a blend of solitary practise and group effort, a student must explore personal ego as it responds to both forms of Priest/esshood. Training provides an awareness of group working from very early stages yet also promotes the development of the ability to work solitary. The learning of interactive skills through group ritual provides excellent insight into one's self.

Background reading ranges from works of fiction such as the Caldecott trilogy (referred to in the chapter Dancing in the Stars) to THE MISTS OF AVALON, both of which provide excellent insights into the training and skills of a magickal Priest/esshood. Students are also encouraged to explore other topics, ranging from translations of the Dead Sea Scrolls to an

unlimited variety of subjects and disciplines. An understan
of the history of modern neo-paganism is necessary, but a
desired is knowledge of the rich quiltwork of divergent
Traditions which spread throughout the world. Among the
most confusing issues for someone new to neo-Paganism is that
met when attempting to find out just what paganism and/or
Wicca might actually be about.

From the beginning, a Novice begins developing communication skills with other students, with the community, and
also with the Divine. The student must learn to move within the
self and to bring back wisdom, to reach out into the Universe
and bring back response. The foundation of teaching skills is
laid when a student begins learning to communicate these
processes to one's church and community. The nature of
secrecy is an often misunderstood aspect of Mystery training,
particularly in these days of neo-pagan networking and
publishing. The nature of secrecy which is described in The
Admonition refers to the specific nature of study within The
Mystery School, not to neo-paganism in general and
metaphysical studies. Although Wicca has become a fairly open
topic of conversation, the Mysteries of a given Tradition remain
the major aspect of that Tradition's power.

Secrecy is a highly effective tool for learning to communicate the Mysteries in the vernacular of those with whom
you are speaking. Early on, one learns to discuss Witchcraft in
phrases which allow for interaction with nonpagans and a level
of comfort in being oneself while among those of potentially
hostile religions. Secrecy causes one to choose words more
appropriate for the ears of the listener. This actually increases
the levels of communication. There are other aspects of secrecy
which come into play.

Even though the flowering of neo-paganism might seem to
have removed the need for secrecy, there remain strong social
reactions against our new-found freedoms. Friendships have
been lost because a new pagan tried to convert an old
schoolmate. Jobs, marriages, family ties are all subject to the

misunderstandings created from Hollywood movies and the popular notion that all of Witchcraft is linked to satanism. No matter how enthusiastic the new Novice, it remains best to wait with explanations until you are better trained, able to provide thorough, well-studied explanations. Yet, secrecy does not prohibit suggestions for books to read, saying I sure thought this was something!.

Students are advised that the boundaries of secrecy are inevitably learned the hard way. It is not possible to establish strict limits upon secrecy. A student must learn to internalize, digest and comprehend the nature of the Mysteries. Only when the time is right can s/he begin to talk more freely of them, for any discussion will be met with doubts and questions which call for careful response. In the meantime, one learns to translate new spiritual awakenings into acceptable vernacular. This can only lead to the foundation of acceptance that we are all children and that all Paths and all religions are inherently good, none above the other, not even our own Beloved Wicca. There are no absolutes in matters of secrecy, yet it has been an aspect of mystery training for as long as humans have perceived the Magick of the Universe. As the Earth is our role model, we must keep in mind that the seed is sown within the Earth, unseen, before it is ready to bring forth the leaves and the bloom.

Among the most difficult lessons to be imparted are those which teach a student to live in the present, freed of past emotions and future expectations. Learning to live in the Tao and to flow with change as a natural mode of being is a complex, sometimes painful process. This is accomplished through guidance, through Quests and lessons, but there is no structured framework which might bring such awareness in any easy fashion. Mental disciplines must be learned. The ability to control one's emotions must be undertaken.

Possibly the most difficult ethic to learn and one which sets our Tradition apart from many others is the manner in which we observe vows of non-manipulation. Our approach to the study of Magick is one which is sometimes considered the neo-Taoist approach. Lothlorien holds that it is the understanding of the Universal Magick which is the goal rather than personal favours gained from its manipulation. We seek the wisdom gained from that understanding. The ability to work the powers of Nature to affect the manifest world may be impressive, but it has been learned that one who lives within the natural order finds all of life's needs met.

And there remain other considerations as well. I could not work my will against the Mother's way, even if She has deemed it time for my gardens to suffer drought. I am not more wise than She and there remains a lesson waiting for my mortal mind to discover. To manipulate the weather may be a mighty thing, but what about those from whom I take the rain? There is a price for every action which goes counter to the natural order, even for a Witch. Sometimes the natural order may require that a loved one encounter a harsh lesson. To interfere in the natural order with a healing may be an act of love. Yet what love is that which stops learning? To protect a child from its lessons inevitably leads to a far more painful lesson at a later date.

This is not to say that we do not work rituals of healing, but they are done carefully, in accord with our neo-Taoist ways. With children we create ways in which they are able to promote self-healing. For adults we make healing energies available to them, but it remains the individual's own work and personal karma which determines the outcome of any sacred work. Because this precept may seem confusing, may I quote the forty-eighth verse from the TAO TE CHING (this translation by Jane English may be found in the reading list):

'In the pursuit of learning, every day something is acquired.

In the pursuit of Tao, every day something is dropped.

Less and less is done

Until non-action is achieved.

When nothing is done, nothing is left undone.

The world is ruled by letting things take their course.

It cannot be ruled by interfering.'

But the most important training lies in developing a solid understanding of the nature of ministry. Great value is had for any Tradition through studying the way in which other Traditions and other religions conceive of and implement ministry. Such a study involves looking at one's culture, social fabric, and communities. It also involves a look into the future.

Chapter IV
Initiation: Rituals of Empowerment

Initiation is a complex process to describe. It ranges from tribal rites of passage to those intricate ceremonies found in ancient Egyptian religions. The roots of initiation are threaded through many, if not all, cultures. Intiation is a means of empowering a Priest/esshood. It has its history in patriarchal religions as well as Goddess-oriented religions and both historical sources are worthy of study. The many guises of initiation exist today from secret societies which initiate new members to youth organizations, for initiation remains an effective means of making special that process of entry into membership. Yet initiation is also a means, when practised as a Mystery, of bringing a Novice through the Mysteries of both life and death and of leaving that awareness forever altered.

To initiate a person is to bring that being through a ritual of transformation. At its Highest Ideals, Initiation is a life-changing event. In effect, it changes the course of events for all of that being's future, including forthcoming incarnations. To initiate a person is to elevate one to a higher level of spiritual responsibility. To initiate a person is to connect one's soul with a heritage of spirituality with roots extending over thousands of years.

Many of the Traditions of the modern Wiccan revival are initiatory in that they prepare a person to undergo a ritual of initiation and consider this an essential process connected with their Priest/esshood. Those who have achieved higher levels of skill and awareness are usually the source for the power and transformation which is given the Novice. This is consistent with the manner in which a Mystery Tradition's hierarchy channels energy from the most pure Kether on the Tree of Life to the most dense Malkuth.

61

There are a number of common elements in many of the Wiccan Traditions. The book, WHAT WITCHES DO, describes one major influence of ritualized customs. Various techniques are combined to heighten awareness, promote a certain level of discomfort intended to maintain mental focus and symbolize certain processes; and the process of sensory deprivation and limitations which, when removed during the climactic portion of initiation, provides a most effective sense of spiritual expansiveness.

Initiation provides a Rite of Passage into the realm of a new manifest personality. It provides the Novice with the opportunity to enact changes within the ego, to effectively alter the manner in which the future unfolds. It is common for a person to embrace a new evolution of identity, complete with a new name to be used in ritual workings, and a new identity which are reborn through the ritual experience. Many of the ritual forms of Initiation have elements which recreate a rebirth metaphor, such as bondage or the use of sight deprivation. It is not uncommon for initiatory rituals to recreate the birthing process as a metaphorical passing from the womb.

Initiation is a ritualization which effects a process of transformation through exposing the Novice to the Magick of the Universe. Remember that Magick means change, and the Magick of the Universe, or that which might be called God in some religions, is neutral. Magick is power, but is neither good nor bad. When Lothlorien's Priest/esshood perform a ritual of intiation, we gather together all of our Initiates who have learned the specific Mysteries of that specific level. The ritual is worked collectively to gather all of the Magick of transformation we are able, and to wrap and cradle the Novice in this Magick. But because there are many forms of Initiation, it would be appropriate to first look at some of them.

Self-Initiation
One of the topics which stirs opinions and debate is the nature of self-initiation and its inherent value. Those who hold

that self-initiation is of small merit are narrow in their understanding of reality. There is nothing which would indicate that transformation may not be self-induced and much evidence to the contrary.

Self-initiation is a process through which one must follow the ritual script as Priest/ess to the Self-as-novice. This script may be found in a text or may be newly created. Ideal in times when one has access to neither peers nor teachers, it is a useful tool which contributes to a culture's development of a strong, experienced Priest/esshood which will eventually provide direct initiation for future members.

There are a number of books which provide excellent service for the student who needs to be self-guided, among them A PAGAN BOOK OF RITUALS. In order to promote self-initiation, one must first gain a reasonable skill at ritual performance and an understanding of the nature of astral reality. One must also have an ability at objectification: as one maintains control over the ritualized process, an active, Yang force, so, too, must one become receptive and give the self's ego completely over to the transformative process. The level of skill required to transcend this dichotomy is, typically, beyond that of the Novice. We are fortunate that the modern Wiccan revival is replete with networking systems extending from one post office box to another, spanning many countries and continents. A serious student might do well to seek out training through this web and, when the time arrives, make the necessary pilgrimage to receive Initiation through a direct ritual from an adept and working group of trained Priest/esses.

While self-initiation can be effective, it rarely has the level of power attained by a well-knit group of highly-trained individuals. Within Asian metaphysics, there is that concept which permeates Eastern teachings: when the student is ready, the teacher appears. More and more modern Wicca is moving into the Age of Aquarius: despite distances, kindred spirits are connecting through the marvels of postal systems, computers and telephones.

wever, there are those who lead solitary paths who are
/ through Initiation by another. The most effective forms
o. self-initiation are those through which the Novice gains
access to an entity who is a highly knowledgeable, trained spirit
guide and who assists the Novice in achieving passage into an
astral reality where a profound transformation and empowering take place. An example will be given shortly.

Initiations of Induction

There are many situations in which a person undergoes
an Initiation in order to become a member of a group or
organization. These range from entry into a coven (such as
described in WHAT WITCHES DO) to admittance into a secret
order or even a fraternity. In most aspects, this may be
considered an induction rather than an Initiation (as discussed
in this text). While many aspects of ritual may be present, the
power is derived from passage out of the known past through a
secret ceremony and into the newly-known future. Such
initiations of induction work exceptionally well when membership is essential before the onset of training. These rites also
enhance the profundity of change and can establish an altered
state of consciousness able to sustain itself beyond the date of
induction. These forms of ritual are not designed to promote as
intense a transformation as do those which train and groom a
Novice over a period of time.

There are many dangers in introducing a person to enhanced and intensified empowerment without first ascertaining
that careful training and preparation has taken place. For that
reason, these forms of initiation may frequently be celebratory
helping mark a before and after without exposing the Novice to
pure Magick. After all, pure Magick is quite akin to chaos. To
take a being and intensify all aspects of life, including all faults,
problems and disorders is irresponsible. It takes skill to handle
increased power. As stated elsewhere, Magick intensifies
everything, whether good or whether bad and dangerous.

Initiation into Adulthood

A cultural, frequently tribal rite, this process transforms a person into an adult and is the (only) acceptable means of achieving socially-recognized maturity in that particular society. The ceremony is conducted by a skilled person who has recognized experience and the wisdom of age. It brings a Novice, perceived ready to leave puberty behind, into the Mysteries of adulthood. Such forms may be as culturally developed as a Bar Mitzvah or as primal as a Quest into the wilds, to seek the protection of a totem animal. Such an Initiation may be the means by which a girl learns the Mysteries of that blood which will now flow with the Moon or it may teach the boy of that Magick which seeks release from his testicles.

Such initiatory processes confer responsibility and are often accompanied by rites which place the mantle of adult work upon willing, young shoulders. The freedoms of a child's play are gone and one now embraces the survival of one's peoples. In many regions and cultures, power is also channeled into the new adult, instilling the process of transformation.

Astral Initiations

To introduce the concept of astral initiation, let me relate a personal experience. Nearly a decade ago I was in the midst of several years of highly intensive astral disciplines. At the same period of time I was undergoing an astrological period of change (celestial Saturn moving conjunct a natal Jupiter/Uranus conjuct) and was on the verge of radically changing the Wiccan Tradition which I was then teaching. I was about to greatly expand the scope of my Priesthood.

One night I was brought back from the dream state which, itself, is much like the Bardo realm. I was projected into stark realization, facing an astral reality more intense than anything I had previously known or experienced. I found my spirit in a large, formal temple. A Priest entered, an aged man who seemed to embody the third aspect of the God. I can only describe him as being a manifestation of the lessons and wisdom attributed to Saturn or the masculine counterpart to the Crone. Certainly an awe-inspiring figure, there was that about him which carried the most intense of Mysteries. It was apparent he had transcended most of mortal experience.

When he spoke to me, it was not with words but by placing concepts directly into my mind. He told me he had been waiting for me. His spiritual presence was very strong and it was obvious that he was as wise as the beings of our mythologies or imaginations. I felt no option other than to accept whatever was to unfold.

Placed before the altar, I was made to wait as other beings (in human form) entered the temple and formed a Circle around the central altar — and around myself and this Priest. The ritual already underway; it built to a highly controlled climax. The Priest drew his ritual blade and thrust it directly at my being.

My training, received from my mortal teachers, was very sound. My mind instantly processed all possible information and experience, and I knew no alternative: perfectly still, I opened my mind to growth and change. The knife but grazed my body and the temple was filled with a sense of my having passed a great ordeal. As my mind opened to this astral Priest's thoughts, it was not just his mind entering mine but my mind also entered his. It affirmed the Mystery which teaches that all action is, ultimately, a Circle so aptly demonstrated by the symbol of the Tai Ch'i, in which Yin and Yang perpetually create each other. Our thoughts merged and I was given my direction. Upon returning to this incarnate reality, I set about the work necessary to establish the Mystery School and continue the creation of the Tradition of Lothlorien.

While this may seem like an amazing story to some, I know of others who have undergone other versions of astral initiation: being taken to sacred sites, undergoing rituals of death and rebirth, and returning to incarnate reality greatly changed with their work laid out before them. Such guidance is given to many, regardless of religious denomination or of Tradition.

An astral initiation takes place in the astral but remains as real as any incarnate experience. Magick teaches, As above, so below. To be deemed worthy by the gods, one must have achieved skills which entitle one to be elevated to a new level of work and experience. One must have attained skill at maneuvering within the astral reality and in maintaining a strict mental awareness. And one must be capable of differentiation between the realities and the illusions found in the Bardo state. The Novice must be capable of increasing her/his workload, able to handle the growing responsibilities which accompany the status of an Initiate. Without the presence of a mentor or guide to assist in times of difficulty, the solitaire who seeks astral initiation must usually be even more spiritually developed and self-controlled than the Novice who is receiving Initiation from incarnate teachers.

Initiation at Death

Death may also provide a form of initiation as we pass from one state of being to another. In fact, death holds the opportunity for the greats act of Initiation. W.Y. Evans-Wentz writes, in his preface to the second edition of THE TIBETAN BOOK OF THE DEAD, "to those who have passed through the secret experience of pre-mortem death, right dying is initiation, conferring, as does the initiatory death-rite, the power to control consciously the process of death and regeneration." Because this aspect of entry into the Bardo realm will be dealt with at great length in its own chapter, let us move on in the discussion of Initiation.

The Tools of Initiation

There are a large number of common elements among initiation rituals. These are found not only within Wicca but in many diverse cultures. Perhaps the most common is oath-taking. In a setting designed to promote awe and seriousness, one makes a covenant before witnesses and, frequently, as a written contract. The Novice swears to a specified code of ethics, to proscribed customs and rituals; and to aspire to certain goals and ideals. Such oaths are made in covenant with the Universe, most generally in accord with the specific deification of the Divine which that group recognizes.

Thus the Initiate has given her or his most sacred word to the God/desses and has made a covenant with the Priest/esshood of that Tradition and with one's peers. A tenet of Wicca being, a Witch is only as good as one's word, such an oath-taking serves to dramatically reinforce the process of empowerment.

Sensory deprivation is highly effective in recreations of birthing. My neo-Alexandrian initiation brought me into the Craft with one cord bound about my ankle as a binding commitment to continue upon this journey; and with a second cord about my waist, yoking my higher (spiritual and intellectual) and lower (sensual and primal) selves together. But the third cord, which bound my wrists and suspended them behind my back and from my neck, deprived me of the sense of independence. It inhibited the extension of tactile awareness, of control over independant movement and the ability to determine action. The deprivation of motion promotes discomfort and ought to lead to the acceptance of such a state and the transcendance of that discomfort, lest the distraction inhibit one's ability to be brought into the Circle. The removal of these constraints, later in the ritual, is used by some Traditions as a symbol of liberation, achieved at the birth of the new Priest/ess and the release of any bondage to the past.

The above-mentioned cords are also used to represent the binding nature of oath-taking, the level of commitment to one's path and the reality of one's word. Cords given through Initiation are the cingulum of a religious sect or religious order and are often worn when working among the community: an ever-present reminder that one is an Initiate, a servant and

Priest/ess of the people. These cords may be one's habit (as an adjunct to a robe or even as the only garb) for they represent the fact that one has been bound to the new behavior (habits) of the future and unbound from those of the past.

Sight deprivation is a common tool of initiation rituals for there is perhaps nothing other than darkness which may take one so completely to the womb of inner rebirth. Accustomed to sustained darkness, the candles of a temple are a source of joyful illumination for eyes which have been closed for a major period of ritual work. To the reborn sight, the observation of tools upon an altar, of the setting of a temple, creates a profound and lasting visual impression.

The removal of sight merely deprives one sense. It also produces a fascinating change in awareness: other senses are greatly enhanced. Each word of a well-spoken ritual sounds clear as a bell, stimulating a vivid image within the Novice's mind. The scent of incense is amplified in power, the sound of footsteps communicates more than one imagines. The Novice has access to many perceptions and insights through greatly expanded sensory awareness.

Although many Traditions would bring you through initiatory rebirth in the same clothing as you were born, clad only with the sky and by your cords, there are Traditions which use other forms of disrobe as a tool of Initiation. The ceremony might be the occasion at which a Novice's robe is exchanged for that of a Priest/ess. Or it may provide the theatrical setting in which one is brought face-to-face, for the first time, with the ritual masks and costumes to be used in Inner Circle workings.

Because it is a matter of choice for a Tradition and certainly not universal in its implementation, education within the Ritual of Initiation might be considered a tool. Dion Fortune writes, in THE TRAINING AND WORK OF AN INITIATE, "a certain stage of experience has got to be reached before we are ready for initiation. The bonds of the senses must have begun to loosen of their own accord before we are ready for the great

69

Renunciation of a personal sense of life. This process is one of the functions of the training."

Introduction to the rituals, to the symbols, tools and to the Tradition's Mysteries and meanings is likely to be incorporated into the Initiation. The ceremony includes setting the new Initiate face-to-face with new knowledge, under circumstances which serve to provide increased retention of any memories.

One of the controversial tools of modern Wicca is the scourge. Inherently powerful and useful, scourging is a religious experience found in most cultures and may be almost as old as religion, itself. In numerous religions, it is the most common pain-related path to ecstasy, but one which may be inappropriate under many circumstances and one which creates far more misunderstanding than transcendance. Certainly, the phrase I was taught in the earliest stage of my training, to learn you must be willing to suffer and be purified, remains a constant truth. For many, that statement would encompass the Magick of the scourge.

For other Traditions, the scourge is used to represent the actual pain of rebirth. In my experience, both being scourged as a Novice passing into the Priest/esshood and later being expected to scourge others as a High Priest conducting Initiations, I was personally uncomfortable with the process. I recall that my mind was focused exclusively upon the intensity of the scourge. Whether as the Novice or later as High Priest, the scourge seemed to stimulate thoughts which sounded just a bit like Goldilocks, Oh, that was too soft . . .. that one is too hard . . .. and that one is just right! The scourge seemed to create a mindset of judgement rather than work to set the ego free from self-awareness. In reading the Ritual of First Degree Initiation of Lothlorien, you will see how this issue was resolved. In creating our First Degree Initiation form, I chose to keep the element of physical discomfort but inspiration guided me to a situation considered more conducive to self-discovery.

In most Traditions, Initiates bring with them a new name

and a new sigil, or symbol, which represent their new identity. This may be accompanied by other paraphenalia such as a new ritual oil, a new formula for incense or the ability to now use, in ritual, a tool which is reserved for a certain level of the magickal hierarchy. Yet it remains that the embracing of one's new role in the community is perhaps the most powerful tool.

It is important to consider what the taking-on of a new identity can mean. As a tool to be used in the transcendence of ego it may be unparalleled. Dion Fortune writes, in THE TRAINING AND WORK OF AN INITIATE, "The personality and the things of the senses have to be sacrificed in order that the Higher Self may manifest; there can be no dispute on this point. All the Initiates have declared it to be so. We are inclined to think that, having sacrificed the personality, we shall be bereft of all things. This is because the mind of the West still clings to its habit of believing that the death of the body ends existence. Yet the process of identity-changing is complex. It is not uncommon to experience a sense of loss. No matter how we may idealize and prefer a new, improved self, the old remains our intimate, familiar constant and its demise may surely stir grieving."

Yet another tool exists which often stirs controversy. There are Traditions in which the Novice is to have intercourse with the God/dess, in which the Magick of the Great Rite is learned experientially. The Great Rite, one of the Mysteries common to nearly all Craft Traditions, is present in some form in most Initiatory Traditions but frequently, as with Lothlorien, existing only in symbolic form. A sexual encounter with the God/dess may be a profound ritual experience, but only under those circumstances when it is truly a transcendant experience and is not reduced to human emotions and judgements. Because sexuality remains a powerful tool which may be incorporated into Initiation, there are other techniques available. A Novice might, for example, practise total abstinence for a period of time leading up to the Initiation, turning that desire and energy to the forthcoming transformation, and later returning home to experience sensual ecstasy in private.

The primary tool which effects transformation and empowerment is the actual power and Magick of a working Tradition. Developing as experience grows, this is cumulative by nature. Typically for a serious working group, the nature of transformation increases in intensity over the passage of time which often results in increasing requirements and expanded preparation and education.

Most Wiccan groups work with a concept known as a cone of power. This is a metaphor for the web of energy, woven through dance and sound by a carefully trained Priest/esshood. The ritual space which awaits the Novice is a highly charged, carefully controlled arena of energy. Through mental disciplines and skills of image-working, the nature of the temple is greatly intensified and will affect all who enter. Magick is drawn from the universe through the invocation of archetypes and by the very nature of ritual itself. Through various ritual techniques, the Novice is suffused with power.

The Novice holds within the self an image of rebirth into a new identity. The image of this identity is given power and the process of its manifestation is brought into motion. After time has passed, following the Initiation, this new personality will have emerged and been integrated into reality. The new Priest/ess will then be living significantly closer to the Highest Ideal sought in this incarnation. I would like to share with you the manner in which this empowerment is brought forth in the Tradition of Lothlorien.

In many Traditions, Initiation is a means of recreating one's life in a new, expanded capacity. Using Lothlorien's Ritual of Dedication would be compared to entering one's adolescence. The Ritual of First Degree Initiation brings one into adulthood, giving one the tools and skills it takes to function as a practitioner, one with the maturity and ability to be a Wiccan Priest/ess in private if not in public. The Ritual of Second Degree Initiation brings one to the Mysteries of the parent. One is now entrusted with the growth and care of others. Completing the cycle, one uses Third Degree Initiation in becoming the Crone.

The First Degree Initiation of Lothlorien

Because the Novice is sightless, many of the passages in this ritual form are designed to promote greater aural awareness. As the Novice listens to the passages of the ritual, the text is designed to evoke a certain set of images. This process begins with the striking of a bell, indicating the beginning of the ritual form. As the candle which represents the God, or archetype of the masculine/active half of the Universe, is lit, the following is said:

'By the light of Osiris, by the might of Cernunnos, By the song of Pan and the fire of Karnayna do I bring this candle to flame, that this altar is bathed in light, that the seeker will find the Path.'

The candle representing the Goddess, archetype of the feminine/receptive forces, is then lit with flame brought from the left candle while the following is said:

'By the light of Isis, as Diana draws light from Lugh; In the night of Aradia, by the brightness of eternal love does She take Her light from the Sun. Yet none outshine Our Lady Divine. She is the goal of the seeker.'

The Circle is next scribed by both Priest and Priestess, who use sword and athame. This Outer Circle is prepared, ideally, by a working couple. However, the Inner Circle is where the actual Rite of Initiation is conducted by the High Priest/ess who has been the Mentor for the Novice.

In preparation for the cleansing of the sacred space, the water is exorcised "that it make sacred this Rite of Initiation" and the salt is blessed "with the Magick of the Goddess that this Rite Initiate Your child into the Mysteries of Your Eternal Wisdom."

As the Priestess aspurges the Circle, the Priest reads carefully the words which drift to the ears of the Novice:

'In the mingling of salt and water do we seek the blessings of our Divine Mother. Bless and consecrate this Circle, take this temple into Your Eternal heart. We see our Goddess in the Earth, we see Her in the Waters; She brings us love and thus do we, Her children, love Her. This Circle we aspurge that we be at a sphere between worlds.

'Come and help us guide a child to Thee. Silent, waiting, sits the seeker. Take our Circle out into Your celestial domains that, when freed of bonds and blindfold, this child comes home to the Mother.'

When the Priestess has returned the chalice of water and aspurger to the altar, the Priest takes the censer. As he carries the charcoal and herbs around the Circle, the Priestess reads for the Novice:

'In the mingling of incense and burning coals do we seek the blessings of our Divine Father. Bless and consecrate this Circle, take this temple into Your Eternal Heart. We see our God in the winds, We see Him in the fires; He brings us love and thus do we, His children, love Him. This Circle we cense that we be at a sphere between worlds.

'Come and help us guide a child to Thee. Blinded, hearing, waits the seeker. Take our Circle out into Your timeless domains that, when freed of bonds and blindfold, this child comes home to the Father.'

The Circle is further prepared with candle flame. The Priest carries the God candle and the Priestess carries the Goddess candle, (although we avoid any restrictive role-taking as flexibility is essential to the creativity). As they flame the perimeter of the temple, they chant "Lord and Lady bless this Circle, bring Thy children home." Music for this chant is found in the appendices.

The Circle is next consecrated with the ringing of a ritual bell, thirteen times in all. Other Initiates who are participating in the ritual are now brought in and the Circle and its portals are sealed with both the staff and the wand.

The invocations for the four elements are those found in The Ritual of Lothlorien. When studied, they are a wondrous array of imagery waiting to be recreated in the mind of the blindfolded Novice. Pentagrams are emplaced in each of the four directions and the Circle's power is further strengthened with the staff and bell.

Because the Magick of this ritual is to be worked collectively, the energy of the Goddess is brought forth through The Goddess Chant (see the appendix which contains music and chants). Already seated in a Circle upon the temple floor, the Initiates now all rise and slowly move into the chanting and dancing of The Witches' Rune.

This power is not released but held within the Circle to aid in the transformation of the Candidate. Each Priest/ess attending the rite uses all training of will and imagination to create this effect. The emotions brought forth in the Novice are powerful. S/he is held in rapture, knowing that all power being raised in this Ritual is to be focused within her/himself. The sounds of the final Eko, Eko . . . fade away and are replaced by the soft steps of bare feet walking to the Northeast portal.

Reverie is abruptly broken when a staff thumps solidly three times upon the floor and the postulant is commanded to rise. Having been seated, arms bound behind, it is with somewhat unsteady feet. The Novice's attention is suddenly caught by the sharp point of an athame held to his/her breast:

> 'You are the seeker standing now in the world of mortals. You have petitioned us to take you through the first Initiation into the Mysteries. This is a step beyond life and through death. Upon your sacred word, is this Initiation of your own desire?'

Should a Novice answer with hesitancy or doubt, all would be over, at the least until a later date. The Circle's energy would be released to the Universe and the Novice returned to the world of mortals. Initiation ought never take place without consent and desire from the deepest levels of being, for:

> 'T'would better be to rush upon this blade and perish than to join this ritual with fear in your heart.'

With the Novice's assent and affirmation that her/his heart is readied with Perfect Love and Perfect Trust, s/he is taken by the Priest and Priestess and tugged backwards into the Circle.

The Passage Past the Watchtowers

If one is to be taken along the Path of Wicca to meet our divinities, then surely one may only achieve that pinnacle by having passed through the watchful personifications of the four elements. The concept of Watchtowers is common to many forms of Wicca. From Lothlorien's perspective, they serve the following purpose: if one is to achieve a state of pure energy (a blissful, ecstatic being), it would only be found after the creation of a balanced blend of the four elemental archetypes.

One cannot move into the realm of the Divine without having attained mastery over these four archetypes, which are far more than the representations of physical elements. One cannot achieve a transcendental state without maintaining discipline and control over one's intellect (air). One cannot be set free from manifest realities without a flaming desire for transformation. The watery nature of one's emotions must be given containment and your feet must be firmly planted upon and within the Earth. Inherent in these archetypes is that watchful property which will bring us back to manifest reality should we not be properly prepared. This is what now awaits the Novice.

It is with the Novice her/himself that the Inner Circle is

created. A manifestation of Perfect Trust, the postulant must place this journey in the hands of the Mentor, for together they will walk the Circle of the temple, creating a mandala in their dance. Having been guided several times around the temple, the Novice is brought to stand before the East. The East Watchtower is called forth both by the rapping of the High Priest/ess' staff and this invocation:

'I, Priest/ess and Witch, do call upon the Lords of the East, Protectors of the breeze, Watchers of the wind; I have brought before thee a candidate for Initiation.'

And in one of the most delightful aspects of First Degree Initiation, a voice now appears out of the wind. One of the Initiates has been selected to personify the Watchtower of the element of this quarter:

'Who has been brought forth? Who is it that seeks to bathe in the light of the Goddess and sing the tunes of Pan?'

There are those times, truly, when the theatrics of the four Watchtowers try the inner disciplines of the High Priest/ess, who is on the verge of laughter. Having invoked the most delightful, humorous qualities of the winds, an Initiate creates an awesome sense of power coupled with pure mirth. This Magick is a sight to behold. Yet, the Mentor responds:

'I have come with this Child of the Goddess, who seeks to breathe the fragrance of life, to dance with joy in the Circles of time.'

The East Watchtower asks the Novice for the passwords, that same Perfect Love and Perfect Trust which gained the Novice admittance to the Circle. Pleased that the supplicant knows the words, the Watchtower grants approval:

'So mote it be! You may proceed along this path to meet the Ancient Ones!'

The High Priest/ess guides the unseeing Novice around the Circle, once less than the journey to the first Watchtower. When the Mentor calls upon the Lords of the South, Guardians of the cauldron, Watchers of the fire, it is a quick-tempered voice which responds:

> 'Who has been brought forth? Who is it that seeks to be warmed by the fires of the Goddess and dance in joy to the call of His pipes?'

The High Priest/ess answers:

> 'I have come with this Child of the Goddess, who seeks to find rebirth into spiritual being, to be kindled with the sparks of the Divine Essence.'

The Novice is only given leave to proceed along the Path after having successfully given the passwords, again (!), but also responding to a query regarding her/his motives. Answered simply, the Novice is now led once around the Circle and thence to the West.

> 'I, Priest/ess and Witch, do call upon the Lords of the West, Keepers of oceans and seas, Watchers of the water: I have brought before Thee a candidate for Initiation.'

Responding in a very flowing voice, the West Watchtower answer:

> 'Who has been brought forth? Who is it that seeks to bathe and play in the moonlit waters of Our Lady and feel the tidal rhythms of His song?'

The High Priest/ess responds:

> 'I have come with this Child of the Goddess, who seeks to bathe in the pools of the Infinite, to dance in joy 'neath the Moon.'

To determine the Novice's preparedness (and for a bit of fun), not only are the same two questions asked, but the West Watchtower also asks the Novice if s/he dares to come before the Ancient Ones empty of hand? The wise Novice answers 'I bring an open mind, open to all the joys of the Craft and a love of learning the wisdom of Wicca.' And the Novice is now led directly to the North by the High Priest/ess.

'I, Priest/ess and Witch, do call upon the Lords of the North, regents of the gardens, field and forest, and Watchers of the Earth.'

It is a heavy, solemn voice which calls out from the North:

'Who has been brought forth? Who is it that seeks to dance barefoot on the Mother to the chant of the Woodland God?'

'I have come with this Child of the Goddess, who seeks to breathe the scent of fresh-turned soil, which is the soul of our Mother; and in the proper time return to Her the temple of this body and join those in the Summerland, there to rest before a new life.'

Not only does the North Watchtower ask the same questions, but next delivers an admonishment:

'Before you are allowed to continue upon your journey, I bid you to hear me and take heed of these words: It has been written that if you take but one step upon this Path, you must inevitably arrive at the end: this Path is beyond life and death . . .' Before you take that step, search your heart, listen to your inner voice. You are swearing to a covenant of Perfect Love and Perfect Trust. You are swearing to oaths of secrecy. These are matters to consider. The Wicca have always taken privacy and secrecy as gems of the Mother, to be treasured. Keep our oaths and we welcome you into our Circles and gatherings. Violate these rights and you will no longer be of us. We will no longer trust you and without trust there is no love. Violate our rights and you will be banished. Break your vows and may your weapons turn against you. So mote it be! You may now ed along this path to meet the Ancient Ones.'

ng been admonished to take the forthcoming vows with great seriousness, the Candidate is plunged into chaos. This is accomplished by leading the Novice to the Circle's centre, at which the Initiates are waiting to spin and turn the Novice round and round, midst the sounds of laughter and glee. This provides disorientation and a profound sense of Trust. Out of this mirth a bell strikes and the Candidate is steadied and made to stand still. As the bell continues to toll, the High Priest/ess presents the Fivefold Blessing, kneeling before the Novice and saying:

'Because we recognize the Goddess within you, because we recognize the God within you ... [Kissing the Candidate's feet] Blessed Be your feet which have spent many years walking towards the God and the Goddess, which shall soon dance round many Circles and walk the Path of Lothlorien.'

[Kissing the Candidate's knees] 'Blessed Be your knees, which shall kneel in reverence before sacred altars, to bow down before your Parents.'

[Kissing the Candidate's breasts] 'Blessed Be your breasts, within which is the essence of love, the joy of Infinity: Cherish it well in Perfect Love and Perfect Trust.'

[Kissing the Candidate's eyes] 'Blessed Be your eyes, now closed in seeking, but soon to gaze in reverence upon the Universe.'

[Kissing the Candidate's lips] 'Blessed Be your lips. May they ever chant the praise of our Gods and Goddesses and may all your words be songs of joy.'

At this point the Candidate's measure is taken with red, cotton thread. This is a fairly traditional process, one which involves establishing contractual Trust, for the measure is returned to the Novice, bound around the left arm.

Trust established, the Novice must now endure the pain

and discomfort inherent in rebirth. The Candidate is made to kneel before the altar, arms remaining bound behind the back, and the forehead resting upon the temple floor.

'In ancient days you would have been made to feel the scourge. You may have been forced to face death as a choice. But in the Path of Lothlorien we seek inner revelation. Heed these calls and repeat these vows . . ..'
'I bind myself to the Goddess.'
'I kneel before Her sacred altar.'
'I shall seek the Gentle God.'
'And serve our Lord and Lady.'

There are forty of these vows. Each is signalled with the peal of a temple bell and read by one of the Initiates. The Initiates slowly walk the path around the Circle as the Candidate kneels, bound, blindfolded and with difficulty, before the altar. As each Initiate's voice in turn reads one of the forty vows, the Candidate must give full attention to the words and repeat each of the vows.

Covered are ethical matters ranging from one's endeavor to keep the air pure, even of negative thoughts, to the conservation of fuels; from taking joy in Nature and making a commitment to furthering one's study of the Path of Wicca.

When this process is complete, the Candidate is helped into a standing position and now takes vows in which a covenant is made to help and defend our religion, even in times of persecution; to keep the secrets of our Tradition sacred and to keep secret the identities of those encountered in Inner Circles; and, to be a good Witch, observing the lunar and solar cycles, and continuing to grow.

The vows and oaths complete, the cords are now removed from the Candidate's wrists and ankles and now placed around the waist. The constrictions of rebirth are set free and following the next consecration, sight will be restored. Thus is the Novice consecrated with water and with oil, according to the Inner Mysteries of the Tradition, and the athame, which has been waiting upon the altar, returned in a ritualized manner. There is no longer a Novice, but a Priest/ess.

All feast and celebrate and the new Priest/ess, now a First Degree Initiate, uses her/his athame to acknowledge the Four Watchtowers. This complete, the High Priest and High Priestess banish the elemental pentagrams and the Charge of Lothlorien is read. A symbolic form of the Great Rite is conducted with chalice and athame held over the head of the kneeling figure of the new Initiate. All share in that communal cup and the Circle for the Ritual of First Degree Initiation is closed.

The Ritual of Ordination

The ritual which confers ordination also brings the Priest/ess to the next expansion of The Work. The work of the High Priest/ess includes the responsibilities of a Mentor and those which accompany legal recognition as clergy. This level of Priest/esshood involves responsibilities far greater than the personal, private work of the First Degree Initiate. To embrace one's Priest/esshood at a community level is to make a covenant with the Universe that personal desires and personal gain are sacrificed when the needs of one's people are presented. It would be appropriate to think of this level of work as that of the parent. A good parent is not always popular.

A Mentor must be strict, yet loving but willing to take the less popular role as an emmisary of that which builds the tools of faith and strength. A High Priest/ess must be capable of withstanding tests of faith and weathering the worst of storms. It is a serious responsibility to bring the Mysteries to people, to teach beliefs and yet to question them at every turn. At times it feels a curious Path, but a Second Degree Initiate is brought into the Mysteries of the Motherfather, having passed through the Mysteries of Maturation learned during the period as a First Degree Priest/ess. And the Path before is that which takes the High Priest/ess to the realms of the Crone. Such a constant awareness leads to a demeanor that enables the High Priest/ess to live a religious life, known in the community as a Reverend and comfortable with the fit of that garment.

To be a Reverend, your life becomes a constant role model, although it certainly need not be average. But the High Priest/ess must be capable of providing inspiration to others, to listen to tales of woe and provide counsel and solace, to bolster faith and to absolve guilt. Among the community, having been declared a teacher of the faith, your actions are open to observation. In addition, Ministry at this level involves the creation of sacred space. Having been trained in the manifestation of the four elemental archetypes and having learned to channel Divine Energy through both polarities, one becomes a Priest/ess at all times. The religious life is lived at every moment.

There are many less barriers, now, between the High Priest/ess and the Universe. One must have learned to bend with the wind, to evolve a new direction when the climate is changing. One has learned to bend and shape with the ebb and flow of the Creative Universe. The High Priest/ess knows how to manifest the stability of the Earth and the subsequent lifestyle is one fertile and constantly active.

Living takes place now, never in the future, and life is so full that the past quickly slips from surface memory. One is in constant service with the Children who live upon this planet, no matter what their age. One is in constant service, passing on the Mysteries to those who seek and are willing to learn. Life is a constant devotion to life, an ever-present awe and wonder, a non-ending willingness to do the Work. And the Work is great, for the needs of our planet are endless, and the oaths the Candidate will take are a great and mighty covenant. Despite the joy, there is always that voice which reminds one, This Path leads to the Crone and far beyond this body's death. And it is to that voice that we swear our oaths, for that voice is our deepest self.

Such a covenant is a grave undertaking. There is a joyous element, to be certain, yet such an increase in responsibility must be carefully considered. Such vows are taken in the form of a Covenant Ritual, one which is performed within the sacred space created when the Priest/ess has created the temple through the Ritual of Lothlorien, performed by memory and worked to perfection. The Ritual of Lothlorien establishes the astral temple in which the other rituals are to be worked. A complex ritual-within-a-ritual-within-a-ritual, the Priest/ess is simultaneously working within a number of sephiroth of the Tree of Life and experiencing multiple, astral realities. Once the astral (and physical) temples have been set in place, the covenant is made.

The Covenant Ritual is the creation of the woman who provided me with my advanced Wiccan training. She is a biblical scholar, theologian and therapist and has requested that her identity be preserved in secrecy.

The text of the Covenant Ritual is rich with imagery. Much of it is based upon translations of the Dead Sea Scrolls' passages which contained the Mysteries dealing with Initiation and the passing of knowledge.

The Ritual opens with a passage which describes the fruits of the Spirit of Truth. This text is a statement of belief in a Divine Order which permeates the Universe and is closely based upon the MANUAL OF DISCIPLINE, which is the name for a collection of ten manuscripts found in the first cave. John Allegro's translation would be found in his book THE DEAD SEA SCROLLS: A REAPPRAISAL. Our Book of Shadows' version is read by the Elder who performs the Initiation. These images are used to establish the aura in which the vows are to be made.

'The Law was planted in the garden of the Family of the Wise to enlighten the hearts of men and women and to make straight before them all the ways of true righteousness, an humble spirit, an even temper, a freely compassionate nature, an eternal goodness and understanding and insight, a mighty Wisdom; which believe in all the Works of the God and Goddess; and a confident trust in

Their many blessings; and a spirit of knowledge in all things of the Great Order, loyal feelings toward all Children of Truth, a radiant purity which loathes everything impure, a discretion regarding all the hidden things of truth and secrets of inner knowledge.'

As these images are established, the Candidate for Ordination must affirm a profound belief in the nature of the Universe and its inherent Wisdom and speaks to it thus:

'Thou hast made known unto me Thy deep mysterious things. All things exist by Thee and there is none beside Thee. By Thy light Thou hast directed my heart that I set my steps straightforward upon right Paths and walk where Thy presence is . . .'

At this point, the Priest/ess actually takes those straight-forward steps. This is accomplished by standing over a basin of water (which represents the Abyss) and performing the Ritual of the Lesser Banishing Pentagram. The function of this work is to establish a channel which connects the worlds of the manifest with the realm of the most pure. The Priest/ess uses all experience and training to establish the simultaneous flow of energy and desire between those realms which would pass through the Middle Pillar of the Tree of Life. Thus is the Priest/ess yoked to both worlds, that of the Ancient Ones and that of humans. As a Minister, one is taking an oath to be a servant of both worlds.

When the final chant of the Lesser Banishing Pentagram Ritual has faded, the Elder affirms the joyousness with which one is permeated, having drawn the energies of the Middle Pillar through the body's central chakra system. This text is taken from the same MANUAL OF DISCIPLINE:

'The Law was planted to reward the Children of Light with healing and abundant peace, with long life, with fruitful seed of everlasting blessings, with eternal joy in the immortality of eternal spirit and light.'

85

At this point the Candidate's consecration is begun. S/he is anointed with a mixture of water and wine and given a series of five blessings. As preparation for the journey which is about to be taken, the Candidate's feet are washed. Truly, s/he is being prepared to walk in the radiant presence of the Universal Divinity.

In celebration of having embarked upon this path, the Candidate responds with a passage derived from the Community Rule of the MANUAL OF DISCIPLINE. The complete section be found within G. Vermes' THE DEAD SEA SCROLLS IN ENGLISH. The version in our Book of Shadows is this:

'I will praise Thy works with songs of thanksgiving, continually from period to period in the circuits of the day and in its fixed order; with the coming of Light from its source and at the turn of evening and at the outgoing of light; at the outgoing of darkness and the coming in of day, continually, in all the generations of time.'

The cords of the Second Degree level are now placed about the Candidate's waist and the Elder invokes all of the Mighty Ones, including those of the Higher Priest/esshoods of all religions and the Deifications of the Universe, no matter by what names the many cultures of humans have used to worship the magnificence of existence.

The act of empowerment for Second Degree Initiation is done in a far different manner than the First Degree work. In recognition of the extensive training which the Candidate has explored and in acknowledgement of the personal nature of such an oath-taking, the Ancient Ones are invoked through the Elder who passes on power, wisdom and joy.

Just as the earthly realm of the Candidate will be dramatically changed by this ritual, so, too, is the astral realm. Next follows an astral working, as the Candidate places her/himself into a trance and is guided to a new level of astral work. Although it may easily be believed that the Candidate is given a new astral temple, another perspective is that this realm is merely the same sacred space perceived from a higher sephiroth within the Tree of Life.

The consecration now complete, the new High Priest/ess goes around the altar to the North, proclaiming for all to hear with what ranks among the most powerful phrases and self-invocation of any Priest/esshood:

> 'I am an offering to the ever-living Ancient Ones. I have bathed myself in the tears of many days, a bath well-heated by the fires of my aspirations, a fire well-tended at every phase. I come now, clean and strong, strengthened by the trials, strengthened by the knowledge; I have come many miles and this long journey brings me unblemished and willing, before the altar, ready for death . . . I yearn for the flames to consume me, the flames of my longing for union with Thee. I am a sacrifice to the ever-living Gods and Goddesses.'

Thus does the High Priest/ess cross the Abyss, echoing a very similar call to the Universe found in the Tibetan rituals of Chod, in which death is to be clearly invoked and faced in order to achieve transformation. The final invocations of the Elder and the new High Priest/ess are concluded, and congratulations lead to the feast of the Ritual of Lothlorien. S/he who began that ritual now concludes it, but is no longer the same person.

> 'I will reach the inner vision and through Thy spirit in me I will hear Thy wondrous secrets; through Thy mystic insight, Thou hast caused a spring of knowledge to well up within me; a fountain of power pouring forth living waters, a flood of love and of all-embracing wisdom like the splendour of Eternal light.'

Chapter V
Unions In The Astral Realms: The Ritual of Handfasting

What is a Handfasting? It is a time of celebration, for two people have come together and found mutual joys. They have shared reality, and decided to create a covenant between themselves. Handfasting is a letting go of the past, and a welcoming of the future.

Among the more common Wiccan Traditions is that which calls for the couple to have their wrists bound together with a red cord, for they will be working hand-in-hand. Why red? Perhaps for the same reason that red is the color appropriate for one of the First Degree Initiate's cords. The colour may be associated with passion, and is one of emotion-incarnate, of the magickal brought down to mundane pleasure. Yet, red does not deny the presence of the spiritual, for when used as a ritual colour, it represents a commitment in the earth plane.

A red cord worn around the Initiate's waist represents an important concept: by choosing to take an incarnate Path, one must accept certain rules. The use of a body as a temple for one's spirit requires the sustenance of the temple. We are free to pursue spiritual joys, but must also learn to work within the framework of reality. We must also accept the eventual decline and decay of the body, and we must come to view that complete process as a function of Divine Wisdom. Within the Handfasting covenant, the partners must approach similar concepts and responsibilities.

The red cord which will be bound about the lovers' wrists is a symbol of commitment: promises to nurture and to make as a priority the other's welfare; promises to care for the mundane needs, such as sickness and death; promises of mutual support, including financial, emotional, spiritual, and any other that may be called upon. This cord is to remain in place until the couple has celebrated together the Great Rite following the Ritual of Handfasting.

There is also the lore which calls for the couple to leap over a broom, yet my research indicates that the reasons this folk custom remains with modern Witchcraft is not very consistent. Some believe that this is part of sweeping away the past and clearing space for the future. Others express a belief that this represents a custom to ensure fertility. A definitely minority view is that this represents the Witch's broom and has something to do with the astral. In any case, it is a great source of fun and exuberance, should you wish to incorporate this folk custom into a Handfasting ritual.

There is a tradition which says a couple should be together at least a year and a day prior to Handfasting. Such lore ought give pause for reflection. Handfasting is a ritual form among Wiccan and neo-pagan religions which binds a union. It may or may not be legally binding, depending upon the legal status of the Wiccan Tradition — and the intent of the couple — but it is, certainly, ethically and magickally binding.

To take vows in a ritual space is to establish a Covenant of a most serious nature. By entering Ritual, the oaths are being taken not only before the guests, but within a focused, intensified astral reality. That which is bound in the astral has implications sure to affect future lives. Although modern pagan custom provides for Handfastings of finite duration (the vows may be, for example, for a one year period), any exchange of words and vows must be carefully examined. A promise to love forever, when consecrated astrally, will create a bond extending far beyond this life. Responsibilities taken under oath are set into the very foundations of one's Magickal Being. Swear no words which you are unwilling to keep.

Such oaths are serious promises and for that reason Tradition also asks that the couple has already proven the durability of their relationship (the year-and-a-day-tradition). Does this mean living together? Does this include sexual experience? Such matters are best left to the wisdom of the couple and their Priest/ess or may be determined by the particular Tradition of the individuals.

One of the functions of a religion is that it celebrates such unions with rituals of beauty, to which the family and friends come with a sense of welcome and comfort. This issue, that of welcoming strangers to a Circle, was one of the reasons three years of thought and research was spent prior to the creation the Ritual of Handfasting. It needed to remain very much Wiccan, yet it also needed to be a creation of a magickal (with a small m) environment that would delight and bring pleasure to every guest; one which would also show them that the religious preference of the couple was not a threat, but provided a ceremony reflecting their beliefs and was a work of beauty.

In ancient times, a Handfasting would be a time to put away your weapons. In these days, if there are those present who would be uncomfortable with ritual blades, then it would be appropriate to put away your knives. Should the Ritual be performed in the company of one's kindred, with none present who would be disconcerted at a well-honed athame, then the athame would be appropriate. The Handfasting Ritual of Lothlorien has great flexibility. It may be performed in its most simple state: a lovely piece of ritual theatre that only touches the pagan heart quietly, through poetic imagery of the Divine as an engendered polarity and through its references to the Earth . . .. It may also be performed as a complex work of Magick (with a capital M) performed by one's coven as an Initiation of a union between two persons who are dedicating their relationship to their Priest/esshood.

One of my beliefs is that our families and friends are open to learning about what we do. I would add that they may not recognize this at a conscious level, but any willingness to attend a ceremony which differs from their personal practise is an indication of this openness. They may have no desire to take any steps upon our Paths for themselves, but give them a non-threatening opportunity to see a work of beauty and the words will truly stir their hearts. The ritual which follows does its work for the couple, but the words are written to educate their families and friends and promote greater understanding for the couple's future.

From the very first step of the ritual form the Priest/ess is conscious of working with the energy of everyone present. This is done by creating, with words of poetry and romantic imagery, a sphere of Perfect Love and Perfect Trust. The easiest way to maintain a good sense of control over a public situation is to enhance your ritual with the skills of theatre. Practise your script and move without flaw: you will hold their imagination as a manifest Magick.

The couple will be waiting well outside the area in which the Circle will be created. When they are called to approach the Circle, that walk will represent the Path they have taken which has brought them to each other and thus to this Ritual. The guests will have earlier chosen to stand or sit in a Circle or, if less comfortable, to take places just beyond the circle where one might observe with a good view (and probably a more comfortable chair!).

Prior to the Ritual, the Priest/ess should have spent time with the couple, making certain they fully understand the spiritual implications of making a mutual covenant within a ritual. The ritual consecration of a union places those vows in a sacred trust. It takes the Union itself and empowers it as a form of initiation. It will intensify not only the strengths but also the weaknesses of the Union.

The couple will have acquired Handfasting jewelry. While many prefer a pair of rings, matching pendants or even matching earrings may be perfect. The only limitations upon the Handfasting jewelry are those of the lovers' personal tastes. They have also selected a special candle which will represent the spirit of their relationship. Romantics might choose to light that candle in the years to come at anniversaries, celebrations of the Great Rite, or at times when they are most in need. The couple has also been asked to provide a basket of flower petals.

The flower petals are very important, for they provide us with the means of effectively scribing a Circle, yet with anyone present. Through the subtle we create a sacred space and a treasured memory.

Rituals of union demonstrate another important lesson. We must achieve responsibility in meeting the needs of our communities. Marriage and Handfasting may be synonymous. It is important that we create rituals that our families will enjoy, for a Union is a family event. More than the couple is being bonded. The alternative is for a couple to need two rituals, one for themselves and one for their family. We, as Wiccans, achieve the most growth when we strive for a more complete integration. It would be desirable for any Tradition to create ritual forms which might be performed with nonbelievers present.

In The Rowan Tree, The Handfasting Ritual is performed by a Second Degree Initiate, for a High Priest/ess receives the necessary credentials to file with the government as a legally-recognized Minister of our faith.

The Ritual

The Priest/ess remains before the altar, sitting, kneeling (or standing) until all have become very, very quiet. It is only when everyone is completely hushed that their ears will truly be ready for a feast of words . . .

S/he lights the two, white altar candles, the left and then the right, saying:

> We are all children of the light. Thus do I bring to flame these candles: One to represent the Sun and our Spiritual Father, the other the Moon and our Spiritual Mother. May Their light bring this union of ** and ** to grow in joy and love . . ..

The candles now shining brightly, the Priest/ess takes up the basket of flower petals and reads the following:

> Let your love be as the flowers to the breeze . . . Let it create

93

an ever-growing Circle that spreads love and joy unto the Earth . . .

May you live within a Circle of love and may your Union be a thing of beauty . . .

May your love dance in the eternal circles of time, with the dance of the Earth, with the sacredness of life, and with this temple.

How I love what comes next! A romantic at heart, this simple act never fails to delight me. The Priest/ess now scribes the Circle by scattering the petals. The first time I performed this rite, it was with a full basket of fresh rose petals. (It took two days to remove them from the carpeting). Symbolically and visually, this is a very moving act for neo-pagans and Judeo-Christians alike. If the Handfasting is being performed as High Magick, then it may also be scribed with the athame.

Next, the chalice of water is purified and the bowl of salt is blessed. If comfortable for all who are present, the passages from the Ritual of Lothlorien are read aloud. If the couple is from another Tradition, the ritual script may be adapted according to their preference. At other times (for the comfort of the guests), those words of the Craft are said silently. What is said for the guests, as the salt is sprinkled into the chalice, is this:

Thus are the salt and water blessed, purified and mingled that these lovers shall enter a Circle made clean and pure, able to join themselves together cleansed of all but joy and peace.

The Priest/ess aspurges the Circle. Next, S/he lights the charcoal and blesses the incense. Again, the invocation from the Ritual of Lothlorien may be used, but only when appropriate. The thurible is then held aloft and the following is read:

Thus is the incense made holy and its sacred scent taken round the Circle. The lovers shall enter a Temple filled with blessings: May their life be happy and filled with the riches of love.

The thurible is carried around, the gentle smoke drifting out to stir the imagination of all present. When the Circle has been censed, the High Priest/ess returns to the Circle's centre. S/he takes up the staff and raps it soundly upon the floor (or the ground, if you are working with the sky as your roof). Calling out in a strong voice, the first of the lovers are summoned:

I call upon **. If you desire a sacred and binding union and vows made before us all, come now to the portal.

The first of the lovers comes to the Northeast portal. The staff is again rapped soundly and the call again made:

I call upon **. If you desire a sacred and binding union and vows made before us all, come now to the portal.

Now the second of the lovers comes to the Northeast portal. The Priest/ess brings the chalice of water from the altar and aspurges the feet of each. For this reason, it might be best if the lovers have arrived bare of foot. The chalice is returned to the altar and the censer brought forth. Both are censed and the thurible replaced.

The High Priest/ess brings the couple into the Circle, one and one together, to stand on either side of the altar, one to the East and one to the West. This is a symbolic representation of the three pillars of the Kabbalah. Each lover represents one of the two polarities, and the middle pillar is drawn down, through the altar, to consecrate both their candle and all of the altar: their vows, their jewelry and their future.

The lovers are now directed to place their Handfasting jewelry into a special chalice of clear water which is waiting upon the altar. Each takes up a taper sitting near their respective altar candles. Each lights the taper from the altar candle at hand, and in unison carry the flame to the Spirit candle. That candle is now aspurged and blessed with incense.

Both move towards each other until they come to stand side-by-side to the North of the altar. They take up their Spirit candle and hold it with their hands. As they stand there, the High Priest/ess binds their adjacent wrists together with the red cord. This is the beginning of the consecration of their union. The Priest/ess now takes up the staff and a lit taper, and guides them once deosil around the altar and then to the East.

The Priest/ess lights a burner of incense at the East altar and the yellow candle. In a Craft wedding, the elemental invocations may also be performed. These may be done by the Priest/ess, or by Wiccan friends of the couple. In addition, other elemental invocations may be introduced according to the wishes of the couple. When all of this is completed, the Priest/ess says:

> You begin your journey of life shared, bound together by the vows of this rite; Many are the years you will share and countless the moons you may watch together.
>
> If you keep your vows, your sacred trust, happy will be many of your days.
>
> May the Keepers of the Sacred Winds whisper joy into your life; May you take delight in each other's smiles for all your days unto passing.
>
> Share together rainbows and morning joys. And let your love be as free as the butterfly's flight.

They are guided to the South. The Priest/ess lights a cauldron of fire and a red candle. If other invocations were performed in the East, they should be balanced by the appropriate counterparts in the South and subsequent directions. Then, the Priest/ess says:

> You begin your journey of life shared, bound together by the vows of this rite; Many are the paths you will share and countless the summers you may pass together.
>
> If you keep your vows, your sacred trust, happy will be many of your days.
>
> The past is in these flames. You are forever changed

from this day forward. May the fires of love kindle your passions for each other throughout all your years.

May your love rise anew: an eternal flame to light each day.

They reach the West. The High Priest/ess pours water into a basin or, if freed of walls, upon the Earth Herself. Then S/he lights the candle and says:

You begin your journey of life shared, bound together by the vows of this rite; Many are the dreams you will share and countless the tides of life to ride.

If you keep your vows, your sacred trust, happy will be many of your days.

Share the waters of life, and share the reflection of love in one another's soul. Together explore the laughter of rain, and the mysteries of the Cup of Love.

And in love, share the tears of life.

They reach the North. The Priest/ess breaks off a small piece of the ritual cake (provided by the couple). S/he gives each a small piece to eat. Then S/he lights the green candle and says:

You begin your journey of life shared, bound together by the vows of this rite; Many are the roads you will take and endless the nights of your love.

If you keep your vows, your sacred trust, happy will be many of your days.

Plant your roots together in the Earth yet play in the gardens of life as children and friends.

Grow old together and share a happy home.

The couple are guided back to stand before the altar. Carefully they replace the Spirit candle and kneel before the altar. The important lessons of working together in harmony are well-grasped as they coordinate their bound hands.

Now comes the point of the ritual in which emotion is brought forth as the most powerful of Magicks. The Invocation

rs is read. As the words surround the couple, each is
*n*to the eyes of the other. Each imagines saying the
o the other. Each imagines hearing the other saying the
p. .. This creates a Circle, a holy Sphere of Love with their
own devotion, and should be a most powerful focus of energy
for all present.

The High Priest/ess stands behind them, reading the
Invocation to the Lovers with great care:

Beloved, I seek to know of you, and ask of the Gods/
Goddesses that I be given the wisdom to see you as you are,
and to love you as a Mystery.

I will take joy in you, I delight in the taste of you.

You are to me the whispering of the tides, the seduction
of summer's heat. You are my friend, my Lover.

Grow old and wise with me and I'll the same with you:
A life before us of rainbows and sunsets and a willingness to
share those things of sadness.

I love you.

I adore you.

The High Priest/ess takes the Handfasting jewelry from the
chalice. The lovers now exchange their symbols of union and
express their own vows and words of love. When this is done,
their vows are taken:

Beringed and bound, are you now ready to avow?

The couple answers in the affirmative. At least, that is what
one would expect. If someone gets cold feet at the last minute,
this is the opportune time to avail oneself of the escape
clause . . . However, should things proceed as we believe the
Priest/ess now asks each the following:

**, Do you take your lover and your friend to be your
sworn partner? Will you keep your love and trust, caring for
and cherishing your lover? Will you keep the Promise of
this Rite?

And each, in turn, would answer in the affirmative. Some may prefer to repeat the vow. Others may prefer to use their own words, or to simply say I do.

In Traditional Craft weddings, this is now the time for the couple to leap into the future, and the broom is brought forth. When this joyful custom is done, and all have again quieted down, the Ritual Cup and Cake are blessed and served, and that brings us to that wonderful formality. The Priest/ess now exercises her/his legal powers by saying:

> May we all now pause and reflect upon the beauty of these lovers, of life and of joy.
>
> We all wish the two of you as many days of Perfect Love and Perfect Trust as Life can bring you.
>
> By the legal powers of the State of ** are these sacred vows made manifest.

At this point all guests begin ringing bells. If you wish for a truly glorious sound, make certain that the invitations remind them, or have someone distribute a basket of bells. The couple may hug, kiss, even pose for a photograph.

But wait! Their wrists are still bound with the cord. And so it Traditionally remains until they have gone off and shared the Great Rite. Then is their union truly blessed.

The Great Rite

There are some highly interesting, sometimes problematic but amusing consequences of practising a Nature Religion. The world around us, according to the theologies of Western religions, is a manifestion of the Divine, a creation of likeness. When we observe Nature, it is highly fertile. Wicca is justifiably within that category known as fertility religions.

Fertility religions have a variety of aspects. The fertility of the crops and of livestock is essential. There is also the fertility of the womb, although, since the days in which children were essential to the success of the farm are long past, this is no longer so stressed. Perhaps yet another aspect of fertility may be found in the old folk verse, 'hurray, hurray for the first of May — outdoor loving starts today!' When one sees the Divine manifest in all of life, and that life is rich and abundant with sensual desire, it creates a different view of reality.

The arcane secrets of a religion which include sexuality as a viable means of experiencing Divinity are frequently misunderstood, even, frequently, by the adherents of that religion. Many who practise the tantric sexuality of Hindu and Buddhist religions do so with utmost discretion. And when the potential arises of contact with the unenlightened Western culture, these mysteries are well-kept for the nonbeliever seems unable to conceive of sexual joy as a Divine experience and there are no words which could ever communicate wisely.

Within Wicca, the Great Rite is that phrase which indicates the Sacred Union between the two polarities. The most typical archetypes are those of male and female, being the predominate polarities found in natural life, although certainly not the only alternatives.

There is that union which exists of positive and negative which, when bridged, leads to that dynamic flow of lightning. There is the magickal quality of light when day and night have blended together at twilight. The primary archetypes used in religions are male and female, for it is that Union which leads to incarnate birth. Yet it is essential to not limit our view of the polarities of the Universe, for the Universe extends Itself far beyond incarnate realities.

The cycling of Moon and Sun are a constant form of the Great Rite. Our awareness is of the Full Moon, for then She is bright and the night would be safer. Ancient peoples could gather and celebrate, able to thread their ways through the Woodland. The dark dispelled, evil would be held at bay. Not so at the New Moon, when the dark of night could conceal any activity. Where is the Moon? She is off, conjunct with the Sun. She is being filled with the seed of that zodiacal energy which will wax full over the coming fortnight. On those wondrous occasions when their conjunct is particularly conjugal an eclipse would take place. From the Earth, Sun and Moon appear literally conjoined.

Wiccan and neo-pagan Traditions frequently seek their roots in the folklores which survive in numerous cultures. Folk customs are frequently bawdy, often sensual and replete with sexual innuendo and symbolism. So, too, is Nature. Life is a miracle of ever-constant creation.

The roots of ceremonial sexual union with the Divine are very old. In past cultures, women and men alike were given access to Union with the Divine through sexual intercourse. Many civilizations provided sacred sites where women went to seek intercourse with their god through his priest. Any child so born was considered a gift of the Divine or a son of the God. Such customs existed not only in some of the European pagan cultures which are popularly written into our modern lore but also found practised among the tribal religions of the Hebrews, as late as the time of the birth of Jesus.

The young Christian religion spreading through areas of Europe was, in part, a reaction against the decay of the contemporary religious bureaucracy of old pagandom. The old religions of the day had risen out of the Age of Aries and had become too concerned with money, politics, and were self-serving. Former customs of the Sacred Marriage had frequently decayed into temple prostitution. In those days money bought not only access to the Divine, but might also purchase Divine forgiveness and intercession.

Mythological research will indicate the nature of Divine sensuality. The old myths show that Sacred Unions can take place both for good and for trouble. The difference lies within one's ethics.

It would be possible that the oldest roots of the Great Rite might be found in the power of the village witch. Modern Priest/esses are likely to discover that the longer they practise their Craft, the greater their sex appeal. This has much to do with one's changing ethics. The more one becomes comfortable the self and radiates a sense of joy based upon a positive look, the more attractive one is.

But there is more. The old village witch, mentioned above, whether shaman or wise woman, had great contact with the Divine Power, no matter what it was called. There is an attractiveness found with that Divine Power. Many times I have sat with a student to explain the differences between true love and raw lust. Magick is Magick. It may choose to make itself known through an enlightened thought but it also exists in the ecstasy of that Union within the Sacred Marriage.

And what are those consequences mentioned in the opening of this chapter? Those who embrace the Priest/esshood of Wicca discover that they are found, as time passes, to be increasingly desired. This should not be surprising within the framework of a religion that trains one in the art of channelling Divine Energy, particularly through the symbols of God/desses and of Nature. There is also a natural phenomena in which a being seeks to become conjoined with that complement to its own inherent polarity. The Goddess and the God, as do all deifications, take great pleasure in being adored and loved.

This sensual nature of a fertility religion is never to be an excuse for wanton sex, even though it is stated in The Charge of the Goddess that all acts of love and pleasure are sacred rituals. That quotation also implies the subsequent responsbilities inherent in such knowledge: one must be completely aware and able to manifest beauty and strength, power and compassion, honor and humility, mirth and reverence. It is impossible to maintain these qualities in a base, carnal lust. These qualities elevate the sensual to a level of the sublime and, with proper training, grant access to Divine Ecstasy.

Within the common context and Highest Ideals of the Great Rite, a Priestess channels, with her maximum potential and training, all of the Yin half of the Universe. The Priest, as counterpart, channels the Yang half. There is a natural attraction between these two polarities which seeks union.

One's personal ego must be set aside. One's personality must be placed in suspension. The goal is to elevate one's being to as Divine a level as possible. The implications of this are awe-inspiring when one considers how energies are affected within the astral realities.

It is for this reason that those desiring to explore and experience the Great Rite should pursue extensive training and exemplary disciplines in their lives. The primary dangers of such sacred workings is that the nature of physical reality, of our carnal bodies, is so powerful that one's being will experience a strong, downward momentum to base incarnation or the realm of the Sephiroth Malkuth in the Tree of Life. Such a Path towards the Divine is fraught with the temptations which accompany extreme pleasure and the arousal of erogenous tissue. The potential for abuse of spiritual responsbilities is great. One must be ever cautious, avoiding entanglement in sensate pleasures.

There are Traditions which work with costuming to facilitate the transcendence of personal ego. This may be accomplished with ritual masks, aiding the Priest/ess in assuming the personality of the Divine. There are no formal processes which take place, other than those of a specific Tradition. Within Lothlorien, the Great Rite is performed only in privacy, just as the New Moon is an event unseen. Those Traditions, however, in which the Great Rite may be performed as others witness this sacredness, must be considered with respect and validity. There is much to consider when the release of potent forces through the Cone of Power is shared by a small group who share a covenenant. The two Divine beings are able to place full concentration into their Sacred Union while the Magick is controlled, focused and directed by those of the Circle.

There are occasions in which a deliberate cultivation of sexual tension is present, aiding in the building of the energy of the ritual. Abstinence from intercourse may be used during the period from New to Full Moon. There are also those who would encourage sexual interplay, including intercourse, but refrain from orgasm, using the heightened tension as a means to increase the power of the ritual.

Because there are few guidelines other than ethical issues and the generally accepted belief that the Great Rite should take place only within a Circle cast with adept skill, advice to a student is to proceed with great care. Analysis of one's motives must be thorough. Understanding of one's sexual needs and emotions must be total and complete. Training in ritual and an understanding of mythology is essential.

The astral implications are strong. What is released and worked in the astral will have direct effects upon incarnate reality. A self-serving or (emotionally or physically) abusive sexual act, when deliberately taken into the astral, will do much to cause one troubles and anguish. A bond is created between the participants, one which is likely to survive many incarnations. There is no such thing as a casual Great Rite. One either accepts, fully, all responsibility or one is treading upon a highly dangerous Path.

Yet the ecstasy to be found is Divine. The bringing together of the Divine Polarities, in the most sacred environment possible (that of the Circle), creates a union of energies which explodes, like fireworks, with an infinite array of colour.

Chapter VI
Dancing In The Stars: The Nature And Construction Of Astral Temples

This chapter is dedicated to my dear friend Donna Lyon Rhose

There is a stunningly beautiful concept presented in the trilogy by Moyra Caldecott (see THE SACRED STONES TRILOGY in the reading list found in the appendices). Fascinating characters meet in a stone circle, united by their skills in moving through the astral, and share in ritual and magickal experience.

The word astral is used within our communities far more than it is understood. There are possibly more myths created around the meanings given the word astral than any other aspect of modern Wicca, save for those dealing with the history and origins of some of the new materials. It is first necessary to look at the literal meaning of the word, of which the root, astralis is that of the word for star. Astral, literally, means starlike. Webster's New Collegiate Dictionary provides the following:

> "1a: of or relating to the stars, b: consisting of stars: starry; also 3: of or consisting of a supersensible substance held in theosophy to be next above the tangible world in refinement; and 4: visionary; also exalted."

The concept of a realm composed solely of astral substance may be perplexing to the novice. Certainly it remains perplexing to many who have been around for a long time. The starlike quality of the astral is a perception based upon the property of light. When one perceives the astral existence, one is seeing the light or radiance which both incarnate and discarnate realities project. Some of you may have had the experience of seeing the astral manifestation of a familiar room. It appears as if flooded with light, as if every object in the room is almost glowing with a warm, bright radiance. This is not caused by any changes in either the room or with the objects but rather is perceived because you are looking at reality from the spiritual side of perception rather than the mundane or physically manifest.

There are very few humans, if any, who do not experience the astral side of reality (which is not to imply that they have awareness of the true nature of those experiences). Nearly every human experiences the astral realities during some forms of dreaming. A majority of the dreams in which the dreamer has the ability to fly or to move in a facile, swimming manner may well be remnants of a night-time astral journey taken while the body is asleep. Indeed, a protracted and careful study of one's dreams inevitably shows the spiritual aspects of reality. Dreams of a sexual content are often the conscious attempt to show interaction with someone we know whom is encountered in an astral experience. This statement I ought further to explain. Without the presence of physical bodies, we are primarily energy. In order for two energies to meet and be in communication, the astral experience brings these two entities together more as a form of communion. Both parties meet and, in a manner of thinking, merge. This is a challenging concept to comprehend and one which I caution you about accepting my oversimplified explanation in so literal a manner.

In the TIBETAN BOOK OF THE DEAD, the state of reality which one experiences between lives is called the Bardo state. It is a word used to describe that state of existence between death and rebirth. It is filled with the creations of one's dreams, fears and expectations. It is a place where we encounter the fruits of our labours, the products of our karma. It is often translated in conjunction with concepts of dreaming. The BARDO THŌDOL, as the text is more properly known, is a ritual form which is looked upon as a rite of passage to guide the spirit of the deceased from this life into the next, with numerous points at which the Lama encourages the spirit to seek escape from the Wheel of Death and Rebirth and to pursue the glorious, radiant source of light which is the most divine. There is an important facet of this work which readers of the BARDO THODOL frequently underplay. While many westerners think of this ritual as one performed solely upon death, the introductory passages found in the Evans-Wentz edition carefully, if briefly, point out that this ritual is one which a serious student would perform on a frequent basis during his life.

I include this information in the chapter on astral work, for it shows that the Mystery teachings in Tibet prepare a student for the initiatory experience at death with regular work in the astral realities during life. In the culture out of which the Bardo Thodol was birthed, frequent and dedicated ritual workings are inherent in the training of a Lama. Indeed, the practise of ritual provides one with a gateway to the astral far more easily than one would expect.

A primary difference between Tibetan approach to the Bardo and the Wiccan is that we live in a more kind environment and the Witch is of a Priest/esshood which has a deep love and commitment to the Earth and who looks forward with joy to the next incarnation. I have no desire to escape for I know that I must come here many times and many times again as I make my tortoise-like journey of spiritual evolution.

Another well-known philosophy of astral realities would be found through studying the Kabbalah, for the Tree of Life and its Sephiroth provide a structural means of understanding the nature of realities which range from the most manifest (Malkuth) to the least manifest or that which is pure light (Kether). The study of Kabbalah shows us the manner in which there is a continual motion from unmanifest to manifest at all times, which might be thought of as the equal sign in the formula for the Theory of Relativity ($E=mc^2$). It should be pointed out that the astral realms do not encompass all of the Sephiroth. The astral existence is one which is more light than the reality in which we have been made incarnate, but there remain between the astral and pure energy other realms of a lighter nature.

The realm which we call astral may sometimes provide the common space between the more spiritual realms and our mundane existence. Thus it is not uncommon to encounter spirits, entities, elementals, and a startling variety of creations. Many of the more developed entities which reach towards manifest reality in order to share necessary information do so through the astral. Some of the more notable personalities which are channeled through mediums might be thought of as 'residing among the Sephiroth.'

In addition, those creations which we intentionally and accidentally create with our imaginations also exist in the astral. One might find teachers but one might also find a Unicorn upon which to ride. There is as much variety as one finds in the dream or Bardo state. One of the entities one may find in the Astral is a charming (when he wants to be) blue Unicorn named Andrius. I would like to discuss him as an example of what our magickal imagery creates. Andrius was first created as a literary device for one of The Rowan Tree's newsletters, The Unicorn. Yet in a relatively brief number of years he developed an independant personality and sense of self. Over time, his existence had been further established by those who believed in him, and their belief was not ill-placed. There are stories people have written me of Andrius' appearances to them, including one remarkable event in which he figured prominently in the healing of a young girl. She was among those who deeply believed in Andrius and when her mother called me to say that Michelle was seriously ill and requested healing energies from The Rowan Tree, I suggested that the mother tell her daughter to dream of Andrius that night, and so she did.

Andrius comes and goes and may be contacted by those who both have basic skills of mental discipline (such as meditative) or who have adequate faith. Even if we all quit believing in him, he would continue to exist, but no longer would our belief provide him the sustenance of energy and form which provided him with his birth into the astral. In similar fashion is the astral populated with numerous symbols and creations of all the religions of time, many of which have faded in strength but which continue to exist, for that which is created in the divine has a far greater sense of infinity than incarnate humans realize.

An understanding of the astral realities is essential to any person who desires even the least aspects of control while in the Bardo state. Astral existence is very illusive. It is much the same as dream realities, subject to instantaneous change, to shape-shifting and to responses to our smallest emotional whims triggered by memories, by desires and by fears, among many other functions of ego. The reality of the Bardo state is such that the projections of your imagination (which does not die when your body does) will appear more real than the actual astral existence. Thus, if you die believing you will be going to hell, then hell is what you will experience until such time as your intelligence (which also remains after the body's death) realizes that you are existing in an illusion. I often describe death as dreaming without a body. There are those personalities, found in the astral realities, who exist in a 'dream' reality, caught by the web of their illusion. A Priestess I know suggests that some people may have begun to incarnate before realizing that they have been locked into a sangsaric creation, or illusion. It is for this reason that serious practise be implemented, for clear, conscious awareness of the astral is essential.

There are those who wish to continue their functions as Priest/esses while between lives. These persons will need to have with them the necessary tools of their Priest/esshoods. These tools are mental. They enable one to maintain a firm grasp of ritual archetypes and of certain symbols and images which allow one to return to a predetermined geographical location for one's next incarnation. This is one of the primary functions of an astral temple. Because it exists 'between the worlds' in a very literal sense, it holds the potential of being a sacred space in which we may gather to do ritual, no matter where the participants' bodies are located, and no matter whether those Initiates gathering in the temple are incarnate or discarnate. All that matters is whether or not the mental keys to the temple are firmly held within the grasp of discipline and experience.

In order to work astrally in conjunction with others, serious commitment and disciplined work are necessary. It is for this reason that those groups which desire to work in the astral should study the nature of a covenant and create one together. Webster's dictionary defines a covenant as '1 : a usu. formal, solemn, and binding agreement : compact' and '2a : a written agreement or promise usu. under seal between two or more parties esp. for the performance of some action.' That which is created in the astral by members of a group (or coven) is of so binding a nature that a carefully considered commitment should be taken before any of the work of temple construction is begun.

The Old Testament of The Bible, when read in a more historical perspective without the bureaucratic myths and neo-historical revisions, is filled with stories of covenants between the Priest/esshood and 'God'. It should be noted that many of the early stories were written when the early Hebrews carried the remnants of earlier Priestesshoods, the tribes of which visited sacred wells and other holy sites. Theologically, the construction of an astral temple is a covenant between the working crew and 'God'. It is a commitment to the creation and maintenance of that sacred space, which is being brought into manifestation. It is a commitment to the Divine, to the Godness which manifests in the mundane as both masculine and as feminine and to the 'God' which exists in each of those who partakes of the covenant.

The Nature of Group Work

Is it fair to say that all group workings create astral temples? Perhaps, but perhaps not. Any group which meets over a period of time and has an effect upon natural energy, be it emotion, creation, sensation or other forces, has a profound effect upon the astral. It would be good to consider the nature of astral creation which the countless performances of the Roman Mass have created, as one example of the nature of the 'above' which exists as a result of a group work in the manifest 'below'. In varying degrees this provides us with a means of understanding the results of any group's work. Although their creations may not be a 'temple', it certainly creates 'space'. This effect can be easily perceived by one with skill. Because ritual practise is specifically intent upon effecting change in the spiritual fabric of reality or in transporting one into Universal reality, itself, groups which work ritual are particularly significant. A space created, even unwittingly, by a group who has no knowledge of astral temples remains, even after the group no longer exists. Yet, as an abandoned house, it would slowly fade in strength and stability.

I believe that any group ritual does create an effect within the astral, but the word 'temple' implies an edifice capable of withstanding the changes of the seasons and the pressures of weather patterns. These conditions are no less real in the astral portions of existence.

The importance of carefully constructed astral temples is usually overlooked in modern Wicca. My friend Donna has written me: 'I would have to say, if we expect the Craft to survive, we MUST build Temples and space on the astral — even a whole world in effect. I have come to realize that other religions have done just that, who have wonderful spaces of learning and knowledge. That also effectively helps to maintain their religion here in the manifest world. I have also come to believe that a lack of this very activity is what has put a lot of Wicca onto shakey ground. I've come to really believe in this. This is important if we all wish to survive as a religion.'

As would be true of most ritually oriented groups, Lothlorien has more than one astral temple. Possibly the largest temple which exists is that which was initially defined by J. R. R.

kien in THE LORD OF THE RINGS trilogy. As the journey unfolds in the first volume, THE FELLOWSHIP OF THE RING, the elven Legolas describes the land of Lothlorien, which was the inspiration for the name of the Tradition of which this book speaks. As they journey towards this mythic land, he tells his companions the following:

Lothlorien 'is the fairest of all the dwellings of my people. There are no trees like the trees of that land. For in autumn their leaves fall not, but turn to gold. Not till the spring comes and the new green opens do they fall, and then the boughs are laden with yellow flowers; and the floor of the wood is golden, and golden is the roof, and its pillars are of silver, for the bark of the trees is smooth and grey. So still our songs in Mirkwood say . . .'

When later the entourage actually has made the ascent into the tree, much as we 'ascend' into any Tree of Life, this is what is found:

'The chamber was filled with a soft light; its walls were green and silver and its roof of gold. Many elves were seated there. On two chairs beneath the bole of the tree and canopied by a living bough there sat, side by side, Celeborn and Galadriel . . .. Very tall they were, and the Lady no less tall than the Lord; and they were grave and beautiful. They were clad wholly in white; and the hair of the Lady was of deep gold, and the hair of the Lord Celeborn was of silver long and bright; but no sign of age was upon them, unless it were in the depths of their eyes; for these were as keen as lances in the starlight, and yet profound, the wells of deep memory . . .'

This is not, strictly speaking, a 'working' astral temple. Rather, it is shared with the thousands upon thousands of readers who have found inspiration and romantic vision in this elven vision which so strongly echoes the mythology of modern Wicca. As a conscious construction of a group mind, Tolkien's tree is not a temple yet the author's vision creates the precision which does, indeed, create a specific, sacred space.

It does exist and we do pay it homage, for it has been a role model, inspiration; a Tradition which is strongly herbal, as we have been called, does well to look to the elves. This astral temple is the largest of Circles, of which our Tradition of Lothlorien is but a single star amid the galaxy of all who have found their inner beings stirred by the tales of Legolas and the vision which Frodo, the hobbit, found upon being lifted up the tree to meet the Lord and the Lady.

Where our literal astral work begins is in that temple which is opened to those who have found a sense of magick and wonder in reading a work of ritual theatre which The Rowan Tree has published as a simple, inspiration work. THE HOLY BOOKS OF THE DEVAS has provided many people access to that temple, whether or not an awareness of that poetry's creation of an astral temple actually exists.

The next level of astral temple is that which has been and is sustained by the regular ritual working of The Ritual of Lothlorien, and is open to a smaller circle of beings. As a set of concentric Circles which, from one dimension, create a spiraling cone, we are now led to the next inner Circle. In the Tradition of Lothlorien, this next Circle contains an astral temple which is far more defined, more thoroughly and intentionally constructed, than are the temples of the outer two concentric temples. This astral, sacred working area is known as the Temple of Lorien.

The nature of astral reality is such that all of these astral temples coexist in the same dimension(s) at the same time and space, in the same absence of time. However, the construction of the Temple of Lorien is such that only a rare individual would find access to this Temple. The heart of any temple is the point at which the power is channeled from the Divine. In the context of a Tree of Life or of any sacred tree, this would represent the bole, or core, of a tree. It would also be analogous to the Middle Pillar in the Kabbalah or that point where an image may be empowered to be given the spark of life. In Wiccan terms, this would represent the centre of one's Circle, the point at which the cone of power extends out into the

Universe as a two-directional conduit of Magick.

The path which the Initiate takes to reach the Temple of Lorien might best be described by sharing this work directly from our Book of Shadows. It is presented in an altered form, so that the nature of secrecy and of limited access to our inner mysteries is preserved. It is shared with the hope that you and your kindred are inspired to create your own astral temples.

The Temple of Lorien

The journey to the Temple of Lorien is a long one, filled with many perils. Many set out to reach these sacred stones, but less arrive. One must pass through the outer circles and groves, spending time among the many varieties of trees in that woodland, wondering which is that Tree which will become The Path. Of all those trees for us there is but one, and that is the Rowan.

To learn the Path of the Rowan is to have embraced great difficulty, to have undertaken disciplines and arduous studies, to have let go of comfort in order to have placed one's Priest/esshood before all else. To follow the Path of the Rowan is to have embraced one's Highest Ideals in union with a small group of kindred.

Upon Earth we learn to follow the ways of Lothlorien. Because our Priest/esshood is shared with those not always able to attend our Circles in the flesh, and because our workings are to encircle the Universe, we have created two temples among the stars. The primary of these is the Temple of Lorien. You have seen it in your dreams and you have heard wisps of stories, yet none of them include the secrets it will take to truly arrive at those sacred stones.

Any Initiate is welcome to visit the temple of Lorien, whether one who carries the sigil of First Degree Initiation, that of Second Degree or that of the Elder. Indeed, once within the Temple of Lorien, all are Elders, for within this Stone Circle are we all Magick, having transcended Death and crossed the Sea known as the Abyss. Once you have let go of your physical body you will still come to the Temple of Lorien, for we are told by the Goddess that there is 'reunion with those who have gone before,' and the Temple of Lorien is where our reunions are most welcomed.

There is but one Path and the nature of Lorien is that of Magick. It is possible for two beings to attend the Circle and remain unaware of each other's presence. Only with disciplined training is one able to perceive another in attendance. Yet there will be times when we plan to attend and share in the dancing and then we will know that the others are present. On those nights will the heavens of Lothlorien sing out in joy and will the skies o'er the Rowan Tree be ablaze with star magick.

This journey is best begun from the inner side of a well-cast Circle, though you may also come from your places of rest and of meditation. First you must covenant with us that all dark and worldly energies are kept at bay. Relax your bodies as you have been trained and follow the four levels to your personal, astral temple. There, seek your Tree and take its secret passage, descending down the spiral to your Craft. Within your Craft will you be cradled, blanketed and carried by the flow to seek the Sea. Crossing the Abyss shall your boat come to rest at the shore of the Isle of Lorien. Upon leaving your boat you arrive at a set of steps, reaching in a gentle spiral upwards to the top. There awaits you a plateau, the sacred site. Step with care and be bare of foot for the steps before you are carved of precious stone, able to survive the Ages only when climbed in gentleness of energy and presence.

In the Book of Shadows, the next passages are a careful step by step description of the hand-hewn stairway which ascends the island's central elevation. This is a point at which one establishes various forms and procedures which guarantee that only those who are Initiate Members of the Inner Circle have access. Another facet of this aspect of the establishment of an astral temple is that this stairway is constructed according to very precise detail. Each step has been hewn out of precious stone following precise measurements in cubits.

Although there may be those who are dismayed at the concern with consistency of the images and the commitment necessary to ingrain the measurements & dimensions thoroughly, it is this very aspect of an astral temple which enables it to exist as a private, sacred space which has controlled access. Further, the vividness of detail enable the Priest/esshood to be in accord with the imagery being created. This is a very intense level of making and keeping a covenant.

The first steps are of ivory, carefully pieced together so as to appear as solid blocks, hewn in cubits according to our words. These thirteen are etched with the sigils which represent our solar system: the planets and their relationship with infinity. First is the step with the sigil of Earth, for it is from our Beloved Planet which has begun the journey.

Now you are about to enter the Mysteries. The next step is hewn of Mother of Pearl and the next three are of fine amber. Golden in colour, there are occlusions in each, bits of leaf and flower and upon the third of the amber stones has been encased, in ancient resin, the sigil of the Priest/ess. Then follow five steps of the finest jade, the last of which carries the sigil of the High Priest/ess.

It is in this manner which we collectively follow a path which combines the lore of gems, the magick of colours, and the language of a collection of sigils some of which are common to modern magickal traditions, some of which may be as old as the modern texts suggest and many of which are newly being created and shared only within the Inner Circle. Diligence and skills of visualization enable the individual members of our Inner Circle to literally arrive at the same temple at the same time knowing that we, alone, are those who enter the Stone Circle.

This privacy is easily established. The nature of the number of steps and the patterns of stone and sigil are easily changed, much as one might have the physical lock of a temple door rekeyed. In addition a magickal device has been set in place, the inspiration for which was found in Marion Zimmer Bradley's book THE MISTS OF AVALON. In order to reach Avalon, one was required the spiritual skill of faith, will and training to guide the boat through the mists and attain the island. In a similar fashion, the stairway which has been placed so as to enable the Initiate to ascend the hill has a most singular step.

The thirtieth step is one of purification. Here you stop, and pause, and wait to see if you may continue. From this step there are several paths, but only one will be unfolded to you. Here one awaits, even as the Priestesses of Avalon awaited the raising of the mists. Thus, should someone be attempting entry at a time which should not be, they will find themselves upon a path which brings them a vision of progress: but it is an illusion. They will arrive at a temple of their own dreaming, where they may safely enjoy their magick. But those of us who are of the working Priest/esshood of Lothlorien will move forward.

Standing before you is a Sacred Circle of Standing Stones. Eight are the Stones set into the Mother Earth. Each stands tall, near eight cubits above the ground. Immediately before you is the first stone, which stands to the Northwest. This stone is named Hallows, but only from the Outer Circle. The next stone, rising at the North is Yule, and so on as the Circle continues. Take the path around, marking one hundred and thirteen paces. Stand before the portal and when you have prepared yourself, pass through it.

Walk to the East stone. Stand before it and lean forward so that your forehead rests agains the coolness. Fill yourself with the vision of clouds, of sky and of those images found in our Book of Shadows. Become air in your mind. In like manner commune with the other stones, then walk deosil to the Circle's centre. Face the altar, kneel, bow your head to the soil as you did upon taking your vows. Become One with Lothlorien. Shed the final remnants of ego and embrace your Highest Ideals.

It is after this individual work, sometimes guided by a Priest/ess who conducts us on this astral journey, sometimes done in solitaire fashion after which we join together, that we next perform the Ritual of Lothlorien as a group, do our magickal work, and celebrate, dancing in the stars before following the proscribed return route.

Chapter VII
Entering The Wiccan Bardo:
The Ritual For The Dead

Death exists in the Universe with the same levels of joy and reality as does birth. For the soul which dies free from fear, death is a spreading of one's spiritual wings, the ability to merge into the Dreaming and find rest and recreation before again entering the womb. For those rare Christians who experience that which Buddhists call right dying, death is a gateway to the astral temple known as heaven, filled with the creations of the beloved's religion. Those who die with fear and guilt are more likely to enter other realms which are truly, in effect, astral temples created of the images of hell and of purgatory. No wonder that death, in so much of the world, is considered an evil thing.

Our Western culture clings to sensate reality as a balm against the fear of dying. Death is perceived as the culmination of all of our worst fears. Medicine devotes untold costs to prolonging life. I prefer the way of the Inuit. Give me an iceberg upon which to sit and contemplate the Universe as the Crone's footsteps grow louder. I have no interest in numerous surgeries and gross amounts of chemicals with which to provide me final years spent barely conscious in a nursing home. Modern medicine encourages us to hang on at any cost. I would rather it promoted an understanding and acceptance. But perhaps it is the work of the Priest/ess to teach us to be gracious when the time is placed before us.

Many death anxieties are born of terror instilled in a Christian culture. How many Christians might honestly face death believing that they are without sin? And what has Western culture taught those humans to expect? So many of those who practised their religions faithfully remain terrified, expecting great suffering in a hell of their worst fears after their bodies have died. Can that truly be the gift of the same deity who is called All-Loving? And many others in those same religions continue to doubt that there is any existence beyond that of the body. No wonder there is fear of the unknowable when what our peoples are taught can only fill them with dread. We are not taught to move forward and embrace change. We are not told that a corollary to the deism, 'God is everywhere', implies that our souls, our spirits, do not become extinct at the time of the body's demise.

There are cultures in which religion works to provide the means of escaping the ebb and flow of incarnation. Life in those cultures is, typically, that of hardship, starvation, and deprivation and it is beyond the human potential to wish to return again to such a hell. Yet those same cultures are often those in which the Priest/esshood is known for its ability to exert control over the rebirth process. Within those cultures there are many substantiated cases in which trained teachers consciously choose to reincarnate. There are even dramatic, from a Western perspective, examples, most notably the Tibetan traditions. Yet I seriously question whether escape from the wheel of death and rebirth is truly an option.

Personally, I have no desire to 'escape'. My love for this planet and for all who live upon Her is strong and unshakable. I have worked to develop this love and to make it non-selective, to include those who make me uncomfortable and those who live far outside my ethical and moral reality. There are mountains I have yet to see, oceans to swim in and tides to watch. There are cities I have yet to explore, holy places which call me. And before I can live throughout the world, I fully intend to return to my beloved Mothervalley. Perhaps I shall return again and again until I know all of the Mother's special places on this Earth and can take that knowledge with me into some black hole — Cauldron of the Goddess — to share with the Universe as it passes through the death and rebirth of a new reality.

Many of us believe that reincarnation is a desirable choice. We believe our work is unlikely to be done in one lifetime and no matter how painful the lessons which wait in the next life, one incarnation is insufficient to fulfill a Priest/esshood. I welcome my return. It will take me far more than one lifetime to evolve myself and attain my personal goals before I feel that my share in The Work is complete. Far more time is needed to finish weaving the threads of karma with those who share in my Circles and to snip other threads and take my parting.

If death is a reality, ought we not transform it into a time of spiritual growth? There are role models for us in Asian religions and it is a challenge for modern Wicca to create new role models for the future.

And I am of the Wicca. The thought of returning, according to the lore of Witchcraft, and of holding anew my athame, of reclaiming a Book of Shadows of Lothlorien in a disciplined, loving manner, is exciting. A common mindgame of humans is to sit and daydream about how we would do it differently if we had it to do over again. We do have it to do over again (in our next life) and I, for one, shall. The strength of a Mystery Tradition exists in knowing that the teachers of future generations will be more wise than we. It is exciting to contemplate returning to the same Tradition, able to pursue Higher Ideals than I did this time, to quiet my Virgo self-criticism, which has known all along that an even better performance has been possible. I tell it, 'next life'.

How does one pursue such an intent? By carefully working with the nature of desire and by selecting the images one holds sacred and constant within one's being, one moves along a Path to union with those images. It is this principle which reunites us with those we both love and hate, for their images are yoked to the emotional desire —both good and bad — which link us to those persons. But breaking away from the innate paths to use reincarnation as a spiritual discipline requires training and skill in the arts of visualization and control over one's mind and emotions. The process is enhanced when one lives with the knowledge of the realities of the Universe. Guilt over human failings is destructive. Better one should learn to make changes and continue moving forward with growth and an ever-increasing positive lifestyle. The achievement of goals in one's next incarnation requires keeping those goals constantly in focus and realizing that the work of the Higher Priest/esshood embraces far more than a single incarnation. Thus may one live more free of emotional constraints over the ups and downs of life, for when viewed from the mountain, they are of little significance.

Yet one cannot become so enmeshed in spirituality that sight of the mundane, manifest reality becomes lost. As above, so below. In the same laws, this life affects the next. If you continually work upon improvement and learn from your mistakes, your next life will be inevitably better. If you learn to work within all levels of manifest and non-manifest reality and keep yourself free from excess attachment to those realities, your next life holds greater wisdom than this.

One of the most useful ways to keep pure your Highest Ideals is to be mindful of your next incarnation. For those who work within a Tradition, the images and symbols of that religion ought be as ingrained as any desire. For the Priest/ess, religion is life, lived daily. I am reminded of a phrase I heard from my first Wiccan teacher. He said that when asked why he was a Witch, his response was 'because I can be nothing else.'

The Ritual For The Dead should be conducted by an ordained Minister of the Tradition of Lothlorien of The Rowan Tree Church. Although performed with far less frequency than The Ritual of Lothlorien and other ritual forms, it remains one of our most important rites for those who work as Priest/esses of this Tradition.

Influenced by the Bardo Thodol of Tibet, the Ritual For The Dead may be conducted over a period of seven days, performed for any Rowan Tree Church member, whether or not that member has chosen to pursue the Initiatory Path. The ritual form has been established so that this rite is easily adapted for any person of any belief system, even if not

affiliated with our Church. A Wiccan may, for example,
to have this ritual performed for a family member, as
that relative in moving into the Bardo realm. When perfo...
as a single ritual, this form is of use for anyone who wishes
spiritual assistance.

For Initiates of our Tradition and members of our Church,
preparation for this rite includes not only the legal will, but also
the compilation of what we call a Spiritual Will. A Spiritual Will
is essential in determining the disposition of one's ritual tools.
For example, if one has taken a goblet and, through ritual,
transformed it into a sacred chalice, it has been removed from
the mundane world. The acquisition of magickal possessions
implies a responsibility for all Priest/esses to determine the
disposition of one's sacred tools.

In addition, this ritual form is designed to assist those who
are pursuing the goal of Right Return, or attempting to carry
spiritual training and disciplines into the next incarnation and,
as is believed by the common lore of our Wiccan religion, being
reunited with one's athame and those with whom we share the
expressions of our religion. In the absence of a Spiritual Will,
one's Mentor will proffer advice, but generally one's tools will
be left to the whims of whichever family member has the legal
right to deal with all the property of your estate, whether
mundane or whether Magickal. The Sevenday Rite may also be
performed for Priest/esses of Traditions other than that of
Lothlorien, or for any person who elects to move into the next
realm of being with the workings of The Ritual For The
Dead.

This ritual will be scheduled when arrangements have been
completed with either a funeral home or crematorium. In the
absence of cremation, ashes from the First Day's fire may be
substituted if so ordained in the Spiritual Will of the Beloved.
The term 'Beloved' is used to refer to the deceased person, for it
indicates emotional attachment yet enables us to begin the
essential process of detachment which allows the deceased to
move more easily into the Bardo realm, set free of this reality.

Typically, the ritual will be performed so that the cremated remains enter the Temple on the Second Day of the Sevenday Rite.

The Ritual For The Dead, in its most complete form, takes place over a seven day period, with the burial of the Athame completing an additional 28 day lunar cycle. It is hoped that the power of this rite effectively separates the Beloved from attachment to the Earth plane and sets the spirit upon its journey into the future incarnation(s). That journey will ultimately complete a cycle when the Beloved returns again into this Priest/esshood. Life and Death are all Circles, and this rite is an Initiation into the future.

The printed brochure containing the information given to family and guests contains the following description of the ritual and of the beliefs which it expresses:

> 'It is our belief that Death is a time of spiritual wonder, an opportunity to seek union with the Divine. In this aspect, Death is like an Initiation into a state of religious being.
>
> 'The state of being which follows the death of the body is similar to that of dreaming: the mind continues to experience, to imagine and to create; yet there is no substance, no Earth, for this is the astral (or place of the stars) world of being. It is for that reason that the process of dying is best accompanied by joy and a willingness to send the Beloved off with good wishes for a wonderful journey. This joy is for the coming Union with the Divine Being, the Beloved having gracefully let go of the past.
>
> 'The Rites you are going to experience are filled with the symbols of rituals drawn from many cultures, from the formidable heights of the Himalayas to customs of the Hopis; from the gentlest of Nature Religions to the imaginative imagery of a child.
>
> 'The Ritual will take place as a Circle, for a Circle is the oldest of symbols for the Divine, and within that sacred space will we send the Beloved's spirit into the new life which exists after the body's death.

'You will note that there are two Circles. The Inner Circle is composed of those who are functioning as clergy: the actual Minister and those working in assistance, either the four who represent the elements of Air, Fire, Water and Earth, or those who are the Dancers. These people will be working together to perform ritual theatre which symbolically recreates, in a microcosm of manifest reality, our beloved planet. There will be various activities which take place between the Circles, for this symbolically represents the present state of the soul's being: being somewhat between the worlds of God/dess and of humans.

'We believe that this Rite will assist the separation of the spirit from the mundane world, helping it to free itself of material and emotional attachments that hold it back from Union with the Divine. That journey into Union will ultimately complete a cycle, and the Beloved will again return. For even the seasons turn in Circles, as do all functions of being, of time, and even of death.'

The Ritual for the Dead not only provides a specific spiritual space (a combination of the actual temple and the astral temple) which serves as the focus for the ritual work to assist the Beloved in transformation, but this particular Ritual is one of dance, for dance not only enhances the Initiation into the Bardo but it may also enhance the healing of emotions. Death should be embraced as an act of beauty.

The Ritual
The High Priest/ess should be a member of The Rowan Tree clergy, but the Dancers and Watchtowers may be drawn from friends, family, or from the Novices and Initiates of The Mystery School. All others form the Outer Circle, with adequate space for ritual movement between the Inner and the Outer. It would be desirable that the Outer Circle have seats available for the comfort of guests and family.

The temple and altar are set with the tools of the Beloved and remain in use for the duration of the Rite(s). As the ritual progresses through the Days, tools are sealed and replaced by those of the High Priest/ess who performs these Rites. In addition to the normal tools of ritual, a black candle takes the centre of the altar as does the Beloved's athame. The candle has been dressed with the ritual oil of the deceased.

For those of our training, one of the goals of this Rite is reunion within the Temple of Lorien. The High Priest/ess and those Initiates who are working within the Inner Circle take time prior to the beginning of the public ceremony. The astral Temple of Lorien is established. The Beloved would have spent incarnate time practising the skills it takes to move through the Bardo realm, even following the body's demise, to enter the Temple of Lorien. Thus, this Ritual is actually a celebration held in conjunction with the Beloved's spirit and a sharing of mutual training to facilitate Initiation into the Bardo realms.

* * *

The High Priest/ess stands at the Circle's Centre. All others of the Inner Circle stand at the perimeter, facing inward. The bell is tolled 13 times. [There may be a Bell Dancer, if so designated in the Spiritual Will. If so, the Bell Dancer would both ring the bell and choose the choreography which brings the symbols into manifestation.] The High Priest/ess lights the black candle. S/he then draws the athame and points to the East Watchtower. That person turns outward, and as the High Priest/ess pivots, each person of the Inner Circles turns until all are facing outwards. The bell is tolled once. All members of the Inner Circle draw their athames and slowly move deosil, stepping a slow dance in unison until each returns to their original places: the Circle is now scribed.

High Priest/ess lights the altar candles and recites the invocation for each of the candles. There is a response by those of the Inner Circle.

> A new star shines in the night.
> It is the joyful twinkle in the Father's eye,

> There to bring light to the darkness,
> To warm and make fertile worlds as yet unborn,
> A seed in the cauldron of the Universe.
> Shine brightly, our friend.
> You are now the Sun,
> And He shines now more brightly,
> For you are a candle in the Universe.
> You are truly God.
>
> [*response*] Gone to rest in Father's nest.
> Join the Ancients: You are blessed.

Next, the High Priest/ess lights the remaining altar candle and reads the complementary invocation:

> A new star shines in the night.
> It is a precious jewel in the Mother's necklace,
> There to guard and love Her,
> To join in Her eternal creation of
> The Universe,
> Joined in the Magick of Her Work.
> Shine brightly, our friend.
> You are now a candle in the Universe.
> You are truly Goddess.
>
> [*response*] Gone to rest at Mother's breast.
> You are magick: We are blessed.

The aspurging may be done with the water chalice and salt bowl of the Beloved. The High Priest/ess takes up the chalice of water and places the Beloved's athame into it and reads:

In this Earthly reality, life as we know it emerged from the Great Mother of Waters. She is the Sea, the rising and falling of life . . .

She is the cradle of beginnings, the Cauldron of Cauldrons. And yet She embodies and births all life, regardless of which Path taken. You, our Beloved (name), shall again return, born of these waters. We exorcise these

127

waters of the past, which you desire to let go of; and we bless them with the Highest Ideals of your future.

In some performances of this Ritual, the chalice may be handed to the person representing the East Watchtower, who will insert her/his own athame into the water, to cleanse it, and pass it deosil all the way around the Inner Circle. As this is done, the High Priest/ess reads the Blessing of the Salt:

Beloved (name), you were born of the Great Mother of Waters. Those birth memories live yet within these crystals of salt.

Now are you blessed. Your soul returns to the Earth, life upon life, growing wise and fulfilling the work of the Ancient Ones. The journey full Circle is one of time, even as grew these crystals.

Purify yourself of the past and dance into the future. And carry within you the spirit of your Highest Ideals.

The High Priest/ess breathes lightly upon the salt. It, also, is passed around the Inner Circle. Upon its return to the High Priest/ess, s/he places three measures of salt into the chalice of water and using a small, bound bunch of dried hyssops (ideally, prepared during the Beloved's lifetime), aspurges the Path between the Inner and Outer Circles.

The Priest/ess uses the incense mixture which was the Beloved's. When the herbes have been placed upon the glowing block of charcoal, the thurible is held aloft and the blessing is read:

In the beginning was the breath of the Divine, according to the myths of most religions. The wind of God is the song of the Goddess. The words of creation are the source of endless wonder. Leave behind you this Magick scent: it was created by you in this life and remains here. Let the smoke call forth the breath of the God Which has power only because She awaits Him. Together shall They bring you forth into a new life and then shall the baby cry anew, beginning the first steps to reclaim the Wisdom of the Ages.

The censer is passed around the Inner Circle, each turning in place, creating a dance of Circles.

The Beloved's wand is used to seal the Circle. First, the High Priest/ess walks around the Outer Circle, encompassing all present. As the Inner Circle all turn to face outwards, the wand is presented to the East Watchtower, then passed from person to person. As the wand moves around the Inner Circle, the High Priest/ess reads the following, affirming the role of the wand: that ritual tool which was empowered by the Beloved, to represent her/his incarnate Will.

> You are the wand that seals the Circle. Completing your cycles, you now encompass us from without. You are the Universe which keeps us safe, and you are the power which flows through our Circle.
>
> You are the wand that seals the Circle. Now freed of flesh and pain, the dance you dance is that of Yin and that of Yang, for you now walk in both worlds. You are the Magick that works within the wand.
>
> You are the wand that seals the Circle. You have ended but one dance and have many more before you, for you walk the Path of the Wise. Now journeying where Dreams are but reality, you are the power that becomes the Circle.

Now will the Four Watchtowers invoke the elements. All, save the High Priest/ess and the Four, seat themselves. The High Priest/ess takes the staff and, one by one, focuses all minds upon each of the Four as they do their work. As each of those representing the elements works to become that element, there is also that astral work in which the Four Watchtowers are erecting the elemental standing stones in the Temple of Lorien.

Invoking Air

The East Watchtower lights the East censer (the censer and incense are both that of the Beloved). As the smoke gently fills the Temple, an Invoking Air Pentagram is scribed and the following is read:

> Blessed Be the breeze that carries both the butterfly and the sigh of death . . .
>
> *[The East candle is lit.]*

Should a bird light upon my windowsill, might it be the soul of our Beloved, come back for to share? Let me listen, little bird, to the songs of the Mother that spill from your heart, for within is the voice of wisdom: melodious Mysteries brought from eternity into the present . . .

You have been set free, Beloved (name), and you wear your astral wings like a rainbow: reaching across the worlds . . . The future is a garden, and soon we shall sow the seeds of Spring into your new life. The old we shall take as ashes, and give them to the Mother where She dances round the Stones. They make the gardens fertile, for the past is enrichment for the future.

The new we plant as hopes, as gifts of promise and of love unto the land of Lothlorien . . . And when you return, as you must, the seed will have grown into your Highest Ideals. Taking your athame again into your hand, you shall continue along this Path.

Each butterfly we see might be your soul . . .

[All] 'Blessed Be the butterflies . . .'

[H P/s] Each breeze that carries music might be your smile . . .

[All] 'Blessed Be the breeze . . .'

[H Ps] Even as the wind turns spring into summer, and chases autumn into the chilling deaths of winter, do you now pass through the Mysteries. You are the breeze which give life to the fire . . . You are the bubbles of laughter in the brook . . . You are the song of the Dancing Earth . . .

Invoking Fire

The South Watchtower lights the South cauldron, with (denatured) alcohol from the Beloved's container. As the fire warms and glows, the Invoking Fire Pentagram is scribed, and the following is read:

Blessed Be the fires that both nourish the seed and consume the forest . . .

[*The South candle is lit.*]

Should the fires dance within my cauldron, might they be the spirit of our Beloved, back with inspirations to share? Let me watch with care the tongues of flame, for they dance the joy of Magick's desires, the passions which come from the pursuit of perpetual light . . .

Dance you now within the fires, but we who Circle round must dance outside them. Carry your soul into the sacred flames, leaving behind the past . . . Seek the brightest flame of the Universe, for now you walk without fear into the Mysteries. You hold death yet you also are rebirth. The past is but fuel for the future. Even the woodland suffers the fires in order to survive. New life springs forth from the ashes . . .

The cauldron of the Goddess is the cradle of new life in the land of Lothlorien . . . And when you return, as you must, the flames will have danced into your Highest Ideals. Taking your wand again into your hand, you shall continue along this Path . . .

Each starlight we see might be your smile . . .

[All]   Blessed Be the stars . . .

[H P/s] Each hearth that carries warmth might be your love . . .

[All]   Blessed Be the hearth . . .

[H P/s] Even as the summer's heat is the promise of the longest day, so too the days signal the passing of the Sun. The Mysteries are without beginning and they are without end.

You are the warmth that shimmers Summer air . . .

131

You are the heated waters from deep within the Mother . . . You are the Sun which fuels the Earth . . .

Invoking Water

The West Watchtower pours water into the Western bowl with the tools of the Beloved. As the water's sound ripples through the Temple, an Invoking Water Pentagram is scribed, and the following is read:

Blessed Be the rains that both water the crops and erode the fields . . .

[*The West candle is lit.*]

Should the waters swirl within the bowl of my chalice' cup, might it be the soul of our Beloved, back to sing the Goddess' song? Let me gaze with care into the depths for it will teach the Mysteries of the Cauldron, the depth of that love which transcends both life and death . . .

You flow free, now, through the Universe, even as the waters of time. Dance with joy, now, in the rain-filled clouds, and within the secrets of the oceans . . .

Sail across the Universe, from shore to distant shore. As unfettered as the night, you ride the tides of heaven. Moving easily from the astral veils to the droplets of rain which bathe my gardens, you flow from world to world. Your life is the reality of dreams . . .

Yet, you shall come anew, even as the clouds give forth tears to bathe Lothlorien's Sacred Stones . . . And when you return, as you must, the waters will contain your Highest Ideals. Taking your chalice again in your hand, you shall continue along this Path.

Each falling raindrop might be your kiss . . .

[All] 'Blessed Be the rains . . .'

[H P/s] Each dancing river might carry your song . . .

[All] 'Blessed Be the river . . .'

[H P/s] Even as the falling Summer rains are also Winter's snow, so too do they complete the cycles. Even as the soul comes forth into birth and returns through death do we live the Mysteries.

You are the Moon's reflection upon still waters . . .
You are the droplets aspurged around the Circle . . .
You are the tides of the cauldron . . .

Invoking Earth

The North Watchtower brings forth the Beloved's Pot of Earth. It is brought to the High Priest/ess who implants the Beloved's athame into the soil. Placed back in the North, the Invoking Earth Pentagram is scribed, and the following is read:

Blessed Be the soil that brings forth life and decays death into memories . . .
[*The North candle is lit.*]
Should the seed germinate within my garden, might it be the spark of our Beloved's soul, back to partake anew of life? Let me tend the gentle life with care, for though it rises from seed and passes briefly through the seasons, it is no less an inspiration than a star . . .

Grow you now within the Mother's womb, even as a seed within the Crone of Death grows into life, for life follows death, as death follows life and the Circle is danced unto eternity . . .

The Law of the Universe requires that to live upon the Earth and feel the richness of soil beneath our feet we must also pass through death. To walk among the trees and through valleys is to take, also, time where there is nothing but thought. To walk the Circle of the Earth is to know infinity . . .

But it the Earth within which we set our standing stones, and upon which we set our altars . . . And when you return, as you must, the Earth will again bring forth fruitfulness, and your Highest Ideals will be the blooms in Lothlorien . . . Each flower we see might be your thought . . . All Blessed Be the flowers . . .

[H P/s] Each sacred stone might pave your Path . . .

[All]   'Blessed Be the stones . . .'

[H P/s] Even as last Autumn's leaves pass into soil, and leave
         behind only a memory of the flower's beauty, so too do
         you now set free your body. Dance your soul into the
         Mysteries.

         You are the garden of growing wisdom . . . You are
         the fertile soil for dreams . . . You are the Tree of
         Life . . .

*   *   *

The North Watchtower brings the Beloved's Earthpot
around and to the centre, where the High Priest/ess removes
the athame and returns it to the altar. The Beloved's sword is
taken up by the High Priest/ess who, standing in the center of
the Circle, addresses the temple while turning from the East,
deosil around & back again to the East. As the sword points at
each person of the Inner Circle, that person turns deosil to face
outwards. As this dance takes place, the Invocation to Charge
the Circle is read:

Be thou the Circle: Dance the rhythms of the Universe, for
you are now one with the Stars, with the Sun and with the
Moon.

Seek out the Summerland . . . Set yourself free, even of
the loves which bind you to this life now passing . . . Spread
your wings and fly . . . Let go old pleasures, for new delights
await you.

You are now One with Dreams, and your soul must sail
the Moonlit skies . . . Turn no longer to the Earth but seek
the astral temples. There shall you find the joy of
Lothlorien and there shall you wear your Highest Ideals as
a robe of the finest of Magicks . . . For there is the meeting
place of Love and Joy and Truth. And there are you safe
against any evil . . . And there is the Magick for all time
which we shall raise unto eternity . . .

So Mote it Be!

The Charge of the Beloved

On the first day, the crystal ball is brought into the temple by way of the North East portal, carried deosil between the Inner and Outer Circles, then brought through the North East quarter into the Inner Circle. The crystal ball, or orb, represents the spirit of the Beloved. It has been a major tool during the Beloved's incarnation, brought into many rituals, kept upon one's altar, sharing in dreams, and has been developed as a portal through which one is able to pass between worlds.

This dance is performed by the Orb Dancer, as designated in the Spiritual Will. The Dancer stands at the centre of the Circle, holding the Orb aloft as the High Priest/ess reads the Charge of the Beloved. If the Orb Dancer is an Initiate, with access to the Temple of Lorien, s/he may use the dance to recreate the path spiraling upwards to the sacred stones. On subsequent days the Orb Dancer enters the Inner Circle to take up the crystal ball and dances it between the Circles. There are no limitations placed upon the dance, other than entry into the Circles being through the North East portals and of deosil working of the energy and imagery. All days conclude this Dance with the Orb held aloft at the centre of the temple as the High Priest/ess invokes the Charge of the Beloved:

I am the voice of the Beloved. Mine is the song of the Universe in motion . . . I am the sighing of the wind, the feathered sound of a bird's flight . . . Mine is the rhythm of all hearts; those alive as you hear my words, those passed before me into the Summerland; and those who have yet to walk upon the Earth . . .

I am the voice of the Beloved. My song is that of the starred night, the cry of a baby wanting milk, the dance of a hummingbird who takes nectar from the bloom . . . I am the sound of a cloud gliding across the sky, sailing towards the Mother . . . I am the voice of thunder, giving birth to the sky-fires . . . I am the sound of prayer, and the sound of dying. I am the wail of a baby's first cry; and my name is

135

called when you make love, for I am all words at all times, and I Am Everything . . .

I am the voice of the Beloved. If you listen to a flower break the soil at Spring, you shall hear my song . . . If you listen to the soaring of dandelion fluff in the breeze, you shall hear my words . . . I am the turning of the seasons and the passing of Human Ages, for I am the sound of all life and I Am Everything.

I am the voice of the Beloved. Call upon me with the names of the stars. Know me as One with the Ancients, but no longer may you call me by my old name, for I am becoming One with The Universe . . .

I am a new star in the night . . . I am the gentle drop of rain upon your garden . . . I dance with the Lady and I am the music found within His pipes . . . This is the Ritual of my Death. It is a Feast of Joy, for I leave my tools in your keeping and, as time makes its Circle, I shall be reborn . . .

Ours is the Craft of Wicca. We shall dance in the temples Lothlorien has among the stars. We shall meet again and dance again and love again, for such is the Law.

For now, let me take leave and hold me no longer, for I must be free. I am the voice of the Beloved. Find me within The Universe . . . Call upon me with as many names as there are stars in the sky . . . I am One, I am All . . .

The Sevenday Rites

Following the Charge of The Beloved, the Orb Dancer lowers the crystal ball and moves into dance. The first day's ritual is the Ritual of Parting. If the Beloved has worked with a cauldron, the Orb is used to guide the Cauldron Dancer into the temple. The cauldron is carried around the Circles so that everyone present may place a written wish into it, conveying messages of farewell and joyous blessings for the passage into the Bardo realm.

The dance culminates at the centre of the Circle and the Orb is placed upon a pedestal at the North side of the altar. If the Beloved has been a First Degree Initiate, the red, cotton measure might also be placed into the cauldron. The High Priest/ess reads the following, in addition to any passages requested in the Spiritual Will:

> We place into the fire the proofs of your mortality. Gone are the memories of your incarnate reality, gone are the measurements of your body.
>
> As the Phoenix rises, renewed of flames, are you now the Spirit of the Divine and now soar into the Universe.
>
> This is how we set free the soul of our Beloved to find a new body in which to dwell when the time comes to return anew.

At this point in the Ritual of Parting, all meditate and reflect upon the rites of passage. Songs or readings may be presented by one or more Bards. Family and friends may be invited to present their thoughts on the occasion, or wishes of safe journey for the Beloved.

If the Spiritual Will so directs, this is now the time when old journals or dream-notes are given to the cauldron's fire. This represents the process of setting the Beloved free from the memories and attachments to the past. There are those who have set aside nail clippings or hair cuttings during their lives, or other symbols of incarnate reality which are now to be given to the fire. If the amount of material to be kindled is large, the High Priest/ess may wish to continue the flaming of the cauldron following the closing of the Circle.

During the flaming of the cauldron, it is desirable to have those present join in chant or song, whether through listening or by sharing their voices.

The Ritual of Parting (the First Day's Rite) is also the appropriate time for sealing the Book of Shadows. There are various bits of pagan lore regarding one's ability to return and claim anew one's Book of Shadows. If the Beloved has set forth upon this Quest, then the Book of Shadows is sealed. This is accomplished by the placing of an enveloped sigil between the cover and the first page. In the Tradition of Lothlorien, all tools which are sealed are kept by the Elder of The Mystery School. Our understanding is that by learning the sigil, by making it ingrained in one's being, it should be brought to mind in our next life, having been reconnected with Lothlorien through our work in taking to heart its beliefs and images. Should another being gain access to one or more of our tools, this is considered acceptable and within our understanding of psychic endeavor. It is the Beloved's choice: which tools to set aside for the next life and how to mark them. One might use one sigil for all tools, or one might have each named. The key to success lies in how well we know the names and sigils being used.

Closing The Circle

Beginning with the East Watchtower, each of the Four will follow in turn. The East Watchtower walks once around the temple, between the Circles. During this time, the Elemental Invocation from The Deva Ritual of Lothlorien is read.

And the Goddess breathed gently into the void; And behold, the gentle breezes caressed the soul of the Universe. Thus was born the essence of light, of laughter and cheer . . .

Pan sat alone in the Mother's Woodland. Raising His pipes to His mouth He brought forth the first musick, the wings of song, floating in the airs . . .

May the gentle winds of faith stir your soul into seeking the Mother, as the morning song of the dawning creeps over the horizon of your life, may we all share in the laughing and joy of wisdom and may we float in the winged clouds of Eternity . . .

The East Watchtower returns to the East. The East candle is snuffed. After a pause, the South Watchtower walks the path between Circles and reads the following:

From the warmth of Her maternal goodness did She bring fire to Her children, to kindle in them the sparks of knowledge and the fires of delight . . .

From the Sun we take our warmth, from our Mother comes desire. As the Phoenix rises renewed of flames may we, too, embrace the life beyond this . . .

Our Eternal Goddess is the Cauldron of Cerridwen; may we dance around Her fires in eternal joy . . . May we embrace the fires of learning and kindle within our passion for wisdom . . .

The South Watchtower returns to the South. The South candle is snuffed. After a pause, the West Watchtower walks the path between Circles and reads the following:

From the deep waters of Her eternal wisdom brings She forth the Mystery of Life; and thus does the Initiate take on the Quest of All-Knowing . . .

From the Cauldron of Cerridwen we take compassion and love, moving deep within the Mysteries, we seek inner knowledge . . . May the God Neptune watch over the seeker as the Initiate plunges to the depths of knowing . . .

Our Mother is the Moon's reflection upon rippling waters . . . May we eternally be bathed in Her love . . . May we seek Her calm, Her tranquility, as we travel from shore to distant shore . . .

The West Watchtower returns to the West. The West candle is snuffed. After a pause, the North Watchtower walks the path between Circles and reads the following:

In our quest for knowledge we cross the fields of the Earth Mother and play in Her forests . . . Her pulse is in the gardens, Her dance is in the jungles, and from deep within Her springs knowledge as the fruits of the Earth . . .

Slowly She dances the seasonal rhythms, To the gentle musick of the Woodlands. Pan plays upon His pipes, and She dances in the grasses, among the trees, to the tune of the Gentle Hunter . . .

Our Mother is the Earth and we are Her children: She gives us wisdom. May we seek Her knowledge in the flowers, and in the green things . . . and in the passing of time when we give to Her our souls, She will take our bodies and plant them for Her flowers . . .

The North Watchtower returns to the North. The North candle is snuffed. The High Priest/ess waits until all are calm, quiet, and again focused. The Beloved's Sword is taken and held, hilt down. The closing is read:

Go now until the morrow. Take no sadness in your hearts, for our Beloved has gone with the joy of angels, with the flight of birds and the beauty of life . . . Let these rites be a time of celebration and of love . . . Hold no soul back with your longing . . . Set our Beloved as free as the stars which grace the night altars . . .

Go now. This rite ends in peace . . .

The Remaining Rites

Should there be but a single day's ritual, the Ritual of Parting is followed, adapted to suit the needs of the family and of the Beloved's wishes. For those who have been working the Wiccan Path and have chosen to be taken through Initiation into a Bardo realm to encourage rebirth and reunion with the Path of Lothlorien, the remaining rituals are performed over the next six days.

The Second Ritual is a Ritual of Air. It is at this Circle that the cremated remains would be brought into the Temple. The Orb Dancer holds the crystal aloft as the High Priest/ess departs through the Portals and returns with the Beloved's ash. The Orb Dancer goes to meet the High Priest/ess. Together, they move deosil and all present turn with the dance so that they are constantly gazing at the crystal ball. During this dance, the High Priest/ess reads the Charge of the Beloved as s/he and the Dancer move towards the Circle's centre.

After the Charge, the ashes' container is placed upon the

altar. Next, the Orb Dancer summons forth another Dancer, who is called a Blade Dancer. Should there be any ritual tools, associated with the element of Air, which are to be sealed for the next incarnation, they are now danced throughout the Temple and presented to the High Priest/ess to be sealed. This would include, according to our particular associations, ritual blades and such things as censers. Once sealed, they are danced out of the temple and the Dancer returns with the appropriate ritual tool of the High Priest/ess. Thus, if the East Censer of the Beloved has been used but is now being sealed and removed, then that of the High Priest/ess would be brought into the temple. Thus, there is a ritualized process by which the Beloved's tools are methodically replaced with those of the clergy who are performing these rites.

The rituals for the third through fifth day continue as expected. The Third Ritual is a Ritual of Fire, the Fourth is of Water, and the Fifth of Earth. Some of the possible choices which the Beloved has considered regarding the disposition of the magickal estate may be exemplified with the cauldron. Should the Beloved wish to seal the cauldron, it may remain unused until the next incarnation. Another option would be to request that it be fired on a cyclical occasion, such as each year at Hallowmas. Another choice would be to set the aside the tool sealed, but not for one's next incarnation. The cauldron might be safely kept to be given to a future Priest/ess who has a particular astrological designation, or it might be a gift to the first Novice of a specific year.

What is important is that no tools have been abandoned. One does not quite own or possess one's tools. Through use, the tools of a Priest/ess come into their own being. With some tools a bond is established which will easily transcend time. The more obvious tools would include one's athame, wand, chalice and the like.

The nature of the seal might best be described as a sigil or symbol which is personally designed. It is kept in a sealed envelope and placed with the specific ritual tool during these

not necessary that a person set aside any tools, but it
...tent with our understanding of Magick that such a
would only further our growth.

...he Sixth Ritual, the Ritual of the Sacred Marriage is that
portion of the ritual which enacts the Great Rite as a metaphor
for the coming together of polarities necessary for the spirit to
be reborn. On this day, following the Charge of the Beloved
and replacement of the orb, a couple performs a variety of
dances. Chosen by the Beloved, these dances may include
masks and costume, song and poetry. Various natural Unions
are depicted, such as the interaction between Sun and Moon, or
those of seasonal myths.

Throughout these magickal works of ritual theatre, those
present focus upon the beauty of the two halves of the
Universe. This focus is channelled into the pair of ritual rings
fomerly owned by the Beloved. Within our Tradition, one
acquires a ring for each hand, one representing the Yang, God-
like energies and the other embodying the Yin, Goddess-like
energies. The other piece of ritual jewelry which is Traditional is
that of the ritual necklace. At the culmination of the dance, the
ritual necklace is opened and the rings are placed upon it at
either end, slowly slid to the centre and then joined. Then is the
jewelry sealed and taken to safe keeping.

But the sense of joy and merriment which should
accompany such a festive occasion as an Initiation truly comes
forth on the Seventh Day, the Ritual of Gestation.

Other tools which have been used in this life, not desired
for the next incarnation yet imbued with one's magickal
essence are now given as gifts. Such gifts may range from extra
pieces of ritual jewelry to robes, from tarot books to altar
stones, from chalices to all those things we gather as we learn
the Wiccan dance.

Following the Charge of the Beloved, the Inner Circle
becomes the gathering place for all the Beloved's possessions
being passed on to others. All of the Dancers from the past six
days carry in the gifts. This may include some which have

remained in use during the ritual; candlesticks, for example. The atmosphere is one of an exquisite dance, for the remaining energies and identities of the Beloved are now being given to the Womb of the Universe.

When all is prepared, the person chosen by the Beloved to execute the disposition of the Magickal Estate enters the Inner Circle and the bell is rung thirteen times. Things are given out and pleasantries, shared memories and stories of the Beloved are told in love and trust, mirth and reverence.

When this is done, the Circle is closed. If possible, the athame is taken now to a sacred site and placed within the Earth for a full lunar cycle before being taken and sealed. Then a celebration is to be held, with music, with feasting and with joy, for even though Death has taken away a dear one, we who are of the Wicca believe that there shall be reunion with those who have gone before, and we know that we shall again walk upon our Beloved Earth. How could it be other?

Appendix One:
A Witch's Personal Manifesto

I. I demand these things of myself as a Witch

i   I must pursue my Highest Ideals.

ii   I must strive to elevate my ethics.

iii   I must be as good as my word.

iv   I must demand integrity of myself.

v   I must be willing to suffer for my religion.

vi   I must willingly embrace discipline.

vii   I must develop financial responsibility & independence.

viii   I must be able to pay my bills.

ix   I must pay attention to my diet & intake of food.

x   I must LIVE the Hermetic Principle.

xi   I must respect the astral.

xii   I must approach ritual with great care.

xiii   I must see ritual work as a disciplined art form.

xiv   I must consider seriously the ramnifications of reincarnation.

xv   I must conserve fuels.

xvi   I must recycle whenever possible.

xvii   I must not litter, not even a cigarette butt.

xviii   I must avoid negative energy, even within my own thoughts.

ixx   I must avoid placing blame for any of the events in my life.

xx   I must take responsibility for my ill health.

xxi   I must take myself seriously.

xxii   I must have humour.

xxiii   I must live with my eyes open and my feet grounded.

II. I demand these things of myself as a member of the Wiccan Community.

i   I must support the work of making Wicca a respected religion.

ii   I must expect financial accountability from those groups to which I donate monies.

iii I must stop the mockery of other religions (including anti-Christian sentiment sometimes found in modern neo-Paganism).

iv   I must not support religious plagiarism (such as the teaching of shamanism by those who have never experienced the wilderness nor studied from a real shaman).

v   I must be respectful of all others' ritual forms.

vi   I must separate myths and reality in our history and in our future.

vii I must work to contribute towards a reputable public image of Wicca.

viii I must protest against pagans who use shock tactics in dealing with the public.

ix   I must upgrade standards of Wiccan education.

x   I must support serious research of our religious heritage.

xi   I must demand quality in pagan literature, newsletters and books.

xii I must support the assembling of libraries.

xiii I must not be a religious isolationist and I must work to remove pagan ghetto mentalities from our communities.

xiv I must demand provocative, challenging workshops over entertainment.

xv   I must share my knowledge and skills.

xvi I must make Initiations increasingly difficult, challenging and rewarding.

xvii I must consider the amount of education other religions expect of their clergy when planning Wiccan training.

xviii I must be willing to network.

ixx I must remain in contact with pagans in other places.

III. I demand these things of myself as a Priest/ess.

i   I must prepare for the deaths and burials of our peoples.
ii   I must provide for the future of my consecrated tools beyond my physical death.
iii I must work towards the establishment of legal ministries.
iv   I must provide for children and their education.
v   I must provide for the survival of my Tradition.

IV. I demand these things of myself as a Wiccan citizen.

i   I must promote community service, being of help to all peoples regardless of their beliefs.
ii   I must be willing to be political.
iii I must be a knowledgeable, active voter.
iv   I must respect and utilize the system.
v   I must find value in the political system in which I live or work actively to promote change.
vi   I must be aware of the world perspective.
vii I must extend myself to world poverty and hunger.

A rough draft of these points was first presented at the 1987 Harvest Moon Celebration in Woodland Hills, California, sponsored by The Pallas Society. I offered this material to provoke thought. in no way do I believe this Manifest to offer a set of laws to govern the behavior of others, but by an open discussion of my personal ethics I hope to provoke thought and communication.

Appendix Two:
An Abbreviated Syllabus of the Requirements of The Mystery School

An abbreviated syllabus of the requirements of Tradition of Lothlorien Pathworking through ordination into the clergy (Second Degree Initiation) and into the training of an Elder.

The Novice Supplicant's Requirements
I. A Candidate for admission into The Mystery School must express, in writing, a desire to learn more of Magick and Ritual than what is available through reading and the study of generalized metaphysics.

II. Prior to acceptance into The Mystery School, a student must provide a biographical description of past studies. Highly desired is a background in metaphysical studies, occult sciences, theology or other non-Wiccan subject materials.

III. A Candidate must study the Admonition upon receiving a copy of it. The student must agree to abide by its principles, acknowledging that failure to do so will result in separation from The Mystery School and the Church itself.

IV. A Candidate for the Novitiate will have copied the Ritual of Dedication and will prepare for it with an understanding of the ritual form to be used. A Candidate will bring a candle of the appropriate colour.

V. A Candidate must develop a basic understanding of the potential of the Path of Lothlorien and have an expressed desire to pursue this Tradition. This is assisted by extensive dialogue with advanced Novice and Initiate Mystery School members.

149

The First Ordeal

I. A consecrated Book of Shadows will be examined. It shall contain, among its loving pages, the following Scriptures and Sacred Keys of Lothlorien:

> The Admonition
> The Novice Supplicant
> The Ritual of Dedication
> The East
> The South
> The West
> The North
> The Novice
> The Ritual of Lothlorien
> The Athame
> The Ritual of Consecration of The Athame
> The Chalice

In addition, the Book of Shadows shall contain original material for each of the following Personal Keys:

> The Witch's Pyramid
> The Athame
> The Wicca
> On Being a Novice
> The Four Elements

II. In either your Book of Shadows or in a personal journal, keep notes & a record of all Full Moon and Sabbat rituals you celebrate from the time of Dedication. Be mindful that you are, in some manner, to celebrate each.

III. Bring your unconsecrated athame. Be able to discuss the nature of the Consecration and to interpret the symbolism. Show an understanding of this work as it relates to historical and traditional pathworking. Discuss the use of similar ritual blades in nonpagan religions.

IV. Demonstrate The Ritual of the Lesser Banishing Pentagram.

V. Bring your working model of a Witch's Pyramid. Discuss

your Personal Key and complete your orals with your Mentor.

VI. Contemplate your pathworking and write a paper. Discuss your relationship to the working of ritual, to the God & Goddess, and to your future within the Craft. Discuss any changes your studies have brought you and interpet Magick as it functions in your daily life.

VII. Spend time in contemplation upon the following topics. Be prepared for your orals upon these concepts.

1. Examine your feelings about structured Pathworking. How well does a structured system work for you?

2. The Path you are studying requires that you observe the same ritual forms as other students and embrace certain disciplines and limitations. What functional process enables this method to bring increased individual freedom and growth?

3. What is the nature of spiritual authority? How does a human attain spiritual authority? How should it exist between Mentor and student?

4. Examine the hierarchical structure of The Mystery School. Examine hierarchical structures within Mystery Traditions in general and as hierarchies develop within religion as a whole.

5. How do you describe yourself as a Magickal Being?

6. What are your Highest Ideals? Is this Path compatible with your Highest Ideals? How might it be changed to become more effective?

7. Discuss the nature of religious truth. Is it relative or absolute? Cite examples of religious truths.

8. What is the source of evil? What purpose does its existence serve in the Universe. Under what circumstances are you likely to encounter it? How do you avoid and protect yourself against it?

9. Contemplate your attitudes towards mainstream

religions and to your childhood religion. Reconcile any uncomfortable and negative emotions.

10. How does your use of the word 'Witch' relate to popular images and neo-pagan concepts? How does it relate to historical images and to those images found which exist prior to the neo-pagan revival of the later twentieth century?

11. Contemplate self-healing. In what ways are your studies useful to promote the spiritual healing of inner hurts and wounds from your past? If you have done this, cite examples.

12. Be prepared to discuss the nature of change. Discuss methods through which you might evoke internal and/or external change. How are both of these connected. What is cyclical change? What is linear change? What is Initiatory change?

13. Contemplate your personal attitudes towards masculine and feminine personality traits within yourself as you are comfortable and uncomfortable with them. Discuss the manner in which they affect your relationship with society. Describe them as strengths and weaknesses.

14. Spend time thinking about the vows of secrecy which bind you. You are also taught to be open and honest. Describe the presence of any dichotomy.

The Second Ordeal

I. The Book of Shadows will be examined. It shall contain, among its loving pages, the following Scriptures and Sacred Keys of Lothlorien:

> The First Degree Supplicant
> The Wheel of the Year
> The Sacred Key for each Sabbat
> The Cords
> Candles
> Divination

>   The Charge of Lothlorien
>   The Covenant of Lothlorien
>   The Mythology of Lothlorien

In addition, the Book of Shadows shall contain original material for each of the following personal Keys:

>   A Key for each Sabbat
>   The Goddess
>   The God

II. Demonstrate a system of divination. Show an understanding of the principles involved. Know and explain the history of this system, the care and consecration of the required ritual tools.

III. Bring the cords for your First Degree Initiation. Explain the significance of their manifest appearance.

IV. Prepare the traditional ritual oil used by First Degree Initiates. Bring yours with you. Describe the herbal and magickal properties of the ingredients. How will this oil be used?

V. Demonstrate your ability to use trance as a magickal tool.

VI. Perform the Ritual of Lothlorien, using your Book of Shadows.

VII. Observing the skeletal form, peform ritual solely with dance and non-verbal chant, making use of your incarnate being as a tool.

VIII. Discuss the origins and meaning of both the Name and the Sigil you have selected for your Priest/esshood.

IX. Complete the following tasks to demonstrate your understanding of these Mysteries:

>   1. Meditate upon the sigil of First Degree Initiation. Discuss what you have learned about the symbolism.
>   2. Demonstrate the Hermetic Principle through ritual

example. Be able to demonstrate it in your daily lifestyle. Complete the orals upon this exercise.

3. Demonstrate your ability to manifest each of the four elements both spiritually and in the incarnate world.

4. Complete a community project within the Rowan Tree Church which provides integration between student and community. Do this in such a manner that you leave behind an imprint of your work for the future.

5. Discuss your plans for the silence and fast you will undertake.

X. Complete the following contemplative exercises:

1. Consider your relationship to the Wheel of the Year. What are the implications of ritual observation of Sabbat and lunar cycles? How do they effect the evolution of your relationship with Nature?

2. Study mythology, both traditional and newly created. Be able to complete your orals.

3. Study the planetary correspondences and their symbols.

4. Study divinatory skills and synchronicity. How would you advise a student to avoid using these methods in a superstitious manner?

5. Demonstrate an understanding of these concepts: ritual as a tool; sacred time/space; rites of passage.

6. How does Initiation represent the process of rebirth? What are some of the qualities and practises you will be leaving behind? How does Initiation prepare you for your death?

7. What is your current level of work with trancework, meditation, dreams and similar skills?

The First Degree Supplicant

I. The Candidate will have been given a reading of the Ritual of First Degree Initiation. S/he must be able to compare this ritual form to other Wiccan forms of initiation.

II. All Initiate Members of Lothlorien will conduct oral exams for the Supplicant. In addition to all of the Pathworking, the following will be included:

1. The Candidate's integration into the non-pagan community and the mainstream.

2. The ability of the Candidate to demonstrate characteristics of Priest/esshood, yet maintain secrecy.

3. A healthy balance between pragmatism and vision.

4. A good working relationship with one's Mentor and with other Initiates.

5. Absence or conscious moderation of dependencies.

6. The ability to cope with divergent views.

7. Humour.

8. Ecological awareness and conservationist practises.

9. Truthfulness.

10. Spiritual awareness as integrated into daily living.

The Third Ordeal

I. The Book of Shadows will be examined. It shall contain, among its loving pages, the following Scriptures and Sacred Keys of Lothlorien:

The Ritual of First Degree Initiation
The Initiate
The Descent of the Goddess
The Chalice Ritual
The Hallowmas Ritual of Lothlorien
The Yule Ritual of Lothlorien
The Candlemas Ritual of Lothlorien
The Child of Light Ritual
The Ritual of the Lesser Banishing Pentagram
The Archangels
The Candidate for Second Degree Initiation
The Sigils of Lothlorien
The Laws of Magick

In addition, the Book of Shadows will contain the original material for all of the proscribed Personal Keys.

II. The Skills of a Priest/ess

1. Attend a major Pagan festival or gathering. Write a journalized account of your impressions for a neopagan publication.

2. Practise as a Priest/ess for one complete cycle of lunar and Sabbat rituals. Be able to demonstrate your awareness of cyclical ritual.

3. Schedule, coordinate and perform at least one group ritual for the Church membership.

4. Have a complete collection of the ritual tools necessary for the performance of group ritual. Each should conform to Sacred and Personal Keys and be properly consecrated.

III. Skills of a Mentor

1. Have in your Book of Shadows the Sacred Keys which comprise the Pathworking steps of the Tradition of Lothlorien. Be able to complete your oral exam upon them and interpret the Path of Lothlorien.

2. Describe fully three Traditions other than that of Lothlorien. Perform a ritual from at least one of them for your Mentor and invited guests. Describe both similarities and differences between the Traditions.

3. Develop expertise in your Art Magickal. Teach at least a six week course in your study.

VI. Healing Skills

1. Bring a ritually prepared Fluid Condenser. Discuss its properties, uses, and complete your oral exams.

2. Gather experience in the Art of Herbal healing. Gather this experience among your kindred and through self-healing.

3. Study an additional form of healing. Present a paper to the College of Mentors on this Art.

VII. Demonstrate the Ritual of the Lesser Banishing Pentogram, to perfection, before your Mentor. Be proficient in the production of sound. Show the changes of energy in your aura. Demonstrate your ability to teach this ritual exercise.

VIII. Ritual Skills

1. Demonstrate a working knowledge of the four elements. Know all symbolic correspondences. Demonstrate balance and polarity among them. Know each alone and in all possible combinations with the others.

2. Bring a copy of a complete ritual script for a Sabbat of your choosing. Following Traditional ritual format, write original material and dialogue demonstrating a knowledge of mythology. Following the raising of the cone of power, provide for a channelling of Magick which teaches the Mysteries of that particular Sabbat. Perform this ritual for the Church and complete your orals.

3. Research the Great Rite both in neopagan religions and historically among major religions. Conduct a workshop for Church members.

4. Acquire a working knowledge of Ceremonial Magick through reading, practise and expert guidance. Perform a ritual for the College of Mentors.

5. Demonstrate your ability to invoke the God and to invoke the Goddess.

6. Develop ritual skills as a solitaire; as a coven member; as a Priest/ess working with Novices. Discuss the processes and complete your orals.

IX. Magickal Training

1. Demonstrate your skills at trance-work. Complete a trance-quest at the direction of your Mentor.

2. Through study and coursework be able to discuss and complete orals on astral projection.

3. Establish a working relationship with your Spirit Guide. Discuss and complete orals.

4. Have a familiar. Discuss the magickal aspects of your relationship.

5. Discuss self-analysis. Maintain regular work in your journal. Develop expertise in the use of black & white mirrors for periods of fortnights.

6. Develop the ability to do counselling, through training and experience outside The Mystery School.

7. Undergo a shamanic Dream Quest under the direction of your Mentor.

8. Have your Spiritual Will on file with The Rowan Tree Church. Be able to discuss an understanding of a Priest/ess' responsibilities towards ritual tools and reincarnation.

The Fourth Ordeal

I. The Book of Shadows shall be examined. It shall contain, among its loving pages, the following Scriptures and Sacred Keys of Lothlorian.

> The Wiccaning Ritual
> The Handfasting Ritual
> The Deva Ritual of Lothlorien
> The Ritual for the Dead
> The Great Rite of Lothlorien
> The Ritual of the Descent of the Goddess
> The Lothlorien Wheel of the Year
> The Inner Mythologies of Lothlorien

In addition, the Book of Shadows shall contain original material as required, including a complete set of Sabbat rituals and a ritual form capable of initiating a being into a more evolved reality.

II. Ritual Skills

1. Perform the Ritual of Lothlorien, to perfection, without the Book of Shadows, before the Church membership.

2. Perform the Deva Ritual of Lothlorien to perfection, using the Book of Shadows, at a major neo-pagan gathering.

3. Perform the Ritual For The Dead to perfection using your Book of Shadows, before the College of Mentors.

Conduct a workshop for Initiate members of The Mystery School describing the processes set in motion with this ritual.

4. Perform the Ritual of the Descent of the Goddess for The Rowan Tree Church and guests.

III. Magickal Arts

1. Demonstrate your ability to read auras.

2. Demonstrate your ability to astral project.

3. Demonstrate your ability to banish psychic attack.

4. Demonstrate your ability to perform ritual healings.

5. Demonstrate your ability to transfer consciousness to mineral life; to plant life; to animal life; to human life.

IV. Mentorship Skills

1. Demonstrate a knowledge of each subject and a professional ability in two or more of these Arts Magickal: astrology, tarot, numerology, Kabbalah, I Ching, herbalism, mythology, trancework, colour magick, Craft history, theology.

2. Work with five Novice Supplicants from the time of Dedication through the Ritual of First Degree Initiation.

3. Bring two Priest/esses from the time of First Degree Initiation through Second Degree Initiation. These are to be persons other than those of the previous requirement.

4. Complete trance quests into future time and into past time without the aid of a facilitator. Do so in the presence of your mentor.

5. Have at least two years' experience conducting sessions using the Trance Induction form from the Tradition of Lothlorien. Do this both within the Church and with the larger community. Have one year's experience conducting past life regressions. Conduct a workshop on reincarnation.

6. Have a major portion of your biography written and archived for the Church.

V. Have and know well the tools of an Elder. Each should conform to Sacred and Personal keys and have been in use for at least one year.

VI. Undertake a week of solitude. At the end of it submit a paper which discusses your role within Lothlorien at present; your visions of the future; your relationship with yourself, your kindred, and with the Universe.

Appendix Three: The Mystery School Reading List

A Reading List of the books required for training within The Mystery School of The Rowan Tree Church

A BOOK OF PAGAN RITUALS, Herman Slater, Samuel Weiser, Inc., New York, 1978

A KABBALAH FOR THE MODERN WORLD, Migene Gonzalez-Wippler, Llewellyn Publications, St. Paul, MN, 1987.

ANDRIUS' COLOURING BOOK OF NUMBERS, Rev. Paul V. Beyerl, The Rowan Tree Church, 1979

THE COMPLEAT ASTROLOGER, Derek and Julia Parker, Bantam Books, New York, 1975

DRAWING DOWN THE MOON, Margot Adler, The Viking Press, New York, 1979

ENTROPY, Jeremy Rifkin, The Viking Press, New York, 1980

GUARDIANS OF THE TALL STONES: THE SACRED STONES TRILOGY, Moyra Caldecott, Celestial Arts, Berkeley California, 1986

THE HOLY BOOKS OF THE DEVAS, Rev. Paul V. Beyerl, The Rowan Tree Church, Minneapolis, 1980

ILLUSIONS: THE ADVENTURES OF A RELUCTANT MESSIAH, Richard Bach, Dell Publishing Co., New York, 1977

INITIATION, Elisabeth Haich, Seed Center, Palo Alto, California, 1974

INNER TRADITIONS OF MAGIC, William G. Gray, Samuel Weiser Inc., New York, 1978

THE LORD OF THE RINGS TRILOGY, J. R. R. Tolkien, Ballantine Books, New York, 1965

MAGIC AND MYSTERY IN TIBET, Alexandra David-Neel, Dover Publications, New York, 1971

THE MASTER BOOK OF HERBALISM, Rev. Paul V. Beyerl, Phoenix Publishing Co., Custer, Washington, 1984

THE MEANING OF WITCHCRAFT, G. B. Gardner, Samuel Weiser, Inc., New York, 1959

THE MIDDLE PILLAR, Israel Regardie, Llewellyn Publications, St. Paul, Minnesota, 1979

THE MISTS OF AVALON, Marion Zimmer Bradley, Alfred A. Knopf, New York, 1983

OCCULT SCIENCE IN MEDICINE, Franz Hartmann, M.D., Samuel Weiser Inc., New York, 1975

POSITIVE MAGIC, Marion Weinstein, Phoenix Publishing Inc., Custer, Washington, 1980

THE SPIRAL DANCE, Starhawk, Harper & Row, Publishers, New York, 1979

THE TECHNIQUES OF HIGH MAGIC, Francis King and Stephen Skinner, Destiny Books, New York, 1976

THE TIBETAN BOOK OF THE DEAD, W.Y. Evans-Wentz, Oxford University Press, London, 1960

THE TRAINING AND WORK OF AN INITIATE, Dion Fortune, The Aquarian Press, Wellingborough, Northamptonshire, 1978

WHAT WITCHES DO, Stewart Farrar, Phoenix Publishing Co., Custer, Washington, 1983

WICCA: THE ANCIENT WAY, Janus-Mithras, Nuit-Hilaria and Mer-Amun, Isis-Urania (Publisher), Toronto, Canada, 1981

WITCHCRAFT FROM THE INSIDE, Raymond Buckland, Llewellyn Publications, St. Paul, Minnesota, 1975

WITCHCRAFT TODAY, Gerald B. Gardner, The Citadel Press, Secaucus, N.J., 1974

Appendix Four: Bibliography of Related Reading

ALCHEMICAL STUDIES, C. G. Jung, Translated by R. F. C. Hull, Princeton University Press, USA, 1967

AN ABC OF WITCHCRAFT PAST AND PRESENT, Doreen Valiente, Phoenix Publishing Inc., Custer, Washington, USA, 1973

BLACK ELK SPEAKS, John G. Neihardt, Washington Square Press, New York, 1972

THE BOOK OF CEREMONIAL MAGIC, A. E. Waite, The Citadel Press, Secaucus, NJ, USA, 1961

THE COMPLETE BOOK OF SAXON WITCHCRAFT, Raymond Buckland, Samuel Weiser, New York, 1978

COMPLETE BOOK OF WITCHCRAFT, Raymond Buckland, Llewellyn Publishing, St. Paul, MN, USA, 1987

CREATIVE VISUALIZATION, Melita Denning and Osborne Phillips, Llewellyn Publications, St. Paul, 1981

THE DEAD SEA SCROLLS: A REAPPRAISAL, John Allegro, Penguin Books, New York, 1964

THE DEAD SEA SCROLLS IN ENGLISH, G. Vermes, Penguin Books, New York, 1975

DECEPTIONS AND MYTHS OF THE BIBLE, Lloyd Graham, Bell Publishing Company, New York, 1975

DREAMING THE DARK: MAGIC, SEX & POLITICS, Starhawk, Beacon Press, Boston, Mass., USA, 1982

EARTH MAGIC, Francis Hitching, Pocket Books, New York, 1976

EARTH MAGIC: A DIANIC BOOK OF SHADOWS, Marion Weinstein, Phoenix Publishing Inc., Custer, Washington, 1980

EARTH POWER, Scott Cunningham, Llewellyn Publications, St. Paul, 1984

THE EGYPTIAN BOOK OF THE DEAD, E. A. Wallis
Budge, Dover Publications, New York, 1967
EGYPTIAN MAGIC, E. A. Wallis Budge, Dover Publications,
New York, 1971
EIGHT SABBATS FOR WITCHES, Janet and Stewart
Farrar, Robert Hale (Publisher), London, 1981
THE ESOTERIC ORDERS AND THEIR WORK, Dion
Fortune, Llewellyn Publications, St. Paul, 1978
GARDEN OF POMEGRANATES, Israel Regardie, Llewellyn
Publications, St. Paul, 1978
THE GOD OF THE WITCHES, Margaret A. Murray,
Oxford University Press, London, 1970
GODS, GRAVES AND SCHOLARS, C. W. Ceram, Alfred
A. Knopf, 1968
GOD THE MOTHER, THE CREATRESS AND GIVER OF
LIFE, Lawrence Durdin-Robertson, Cesara Publications,
Eire, 1982
THE GOLDEN DAWN, Israel Regardie, Llewellyn Pub-
lications, St. Paul, 1971
THE GOLDEN BOUGH, A STUDY IN MAGIC AND
RELIGION, Sir James G. Frazer, The MacMillan Co.,
New York, 1950
THE GRIMOIRE OF LADY SHEBA, Lady Sheba, Llewellyn
Publications, St. Paul, 1974.
HEBREW MYTHS: THE BOOK OF GENESIS, Robert
Graves and Raphael Patai, Greenwish House, New York,
1983
THE HISTORY AND PRACTICE OF MAGIC, Paul
Christian, The Citadel Press, Secaucus, New Jersey,
1972
A HISTORY OF MAGIC, Richard Cavendish, Taplinger
Publishing Company, New York, 1979
THE HOLY BOOK OF WOMEN'S MYSTERIES, PART I,
Zsusanna Budapest, Susan B. Anthony Coven No. 1,
Los Angeles, 1979

THE HOLY BOOK OF WOMEN'S MYSTERIES, PART II,
Zsusanna Budapest, Susan B. Anthony Coven No. 1,
Los Angeles, 1980

THE HOLY KABBALAH, A.E. Waite, University Books,
New Hyde Park, New York, 1960

THE I CHING OR BOOK OF CHANGES, Wilhelm/
Baynes, Princeton University Press, 1967

ISIS UNVEILED (VOLUMES I AND II), H. P. Blavatsky,
Theosophical University Press, Pasadena, California,
1976

LID OFF THE CAULDRON, Patricia Crowther, Frederick
Muller Limited, London, 1981

THE LIFE OF PARACELSUS, Dr. Franz Hartmann,
Wizard's Bookshelf, San Diego, California, 1985

MAGICAL RITUAL METHODS, William G. Gray, Samuel
Weiser, Inc., York Beach, Maine, 1980

THE MAGICIAN, HIS TRAINING AND WORK, W. E.
Butler, Wilshire Book Company, No. Hollywood,
California, 1959

MAGIC, WHITE AND BLACK, Franz Hartmann, M.D.,
Newcastle Publishing Company, 1971

THE METAPHYSICS OF SEX, Julius Evola, Inner
Traditions International, New York, 1983

MIND GAMES: THE GUIDE TO INNER SPACE, R. Masters
and J. Houston, Dell Publishing Co., New York, 1972

THE MOON AND THE VIRGIN: REFLECTIONS ON
THE ARCHETYPAL FEMININE, Nor Hall, Harper &
Row, New York, 1980

MOON MAGIC, Dion Fortune, Samuel Weiser, Inc., New
York 1978

MY JOURNEY TO LHASA, Alexandra David-Neel, Beacon
Press, Boston, 1986

THE MYSTICAL QABALAH, Dion Fortune, Samuel Weiser,
Inc., York Beach, Maine, 1984

NATURAL MAGIC, Doreen Valiente, Phoenix Publishing,
Inc., Custer, Washington, 1975

PLANT AND PLANET, Anthony Huxley, The Viking Press, New York, 1974

PRACTICAL HANDBOOK OF PLANT ALCHEMY, Manfred M. Junius, Inner Traditions International Ltd., New York, 1985

RITES AND SYMBOLS OF INITIATION, THE MYSTERIES OF BIRTH AND REBIRTH, Mircea Eliade, Harper and Row, New York, 1965

THE SACRED FIRE: A HISTORY OF SEX IN RITUAL, RELIGION AND HUMAN BEHAVIOR, B. Z. Goldberg, The Citadel Press, Secausus, 1974

THE SACRED PIPE, Black Elk, Penguin Books, New York, 1972

THE SACRED SCIENCE OF NUMBERS, Corinne Heline, New Age Press, Inc., Los Angeles, 1977

THE SEA PRIESTESS, Dion Fortune, Samuel Weiser, Inc., New York, 1978

SETH SPEAKS, Jane Roberts, Prentice-Hall, New Jersey, 1972

SEVEN ARROWS, Hyemeyohsts Storm, Ballantine Books, New York, 1972

SHAMANISM, Mircea Eliade, Princeton University Press, 1964

THE SUN DANCE RELIGION, Joseph G. Jorgensen, The University of Chicago Press, Chicago, 1972

THE TANTRIC MYSTICISM OF TIBET, John Blofeld, E. P. Dutton & Co., New York, 1970

TAO TE CHING, Lao Tsu, A New Translation by Gia-Fu Feng and Jane English, Vintage Books, New York, 1972

THROUGH THE GATES OF DEATH, Dion Fortune, The Aquarian Press, Wellingborough, England, 1968

THE WAXING MOON, Helen Chappell, Links Books, New York, 1974

THE WAY OF THE SHAMAN, Michael Harner, Harper and Row, San Francisco, California, 1980

WHEN GOD WAS A WOMAN, Merlin Stone, Harcourt Brace Jovanovich, San Diego, 1976

THE WHITE GODDESS, Robert Graves, Farrar, Straus and Giroux (Publishers), New York, 1976

WHO WROTE THE BIBLE, Richard E. Friedman, Summit Books, New York, 1987

WITCHCRAFT FOR TOMORROW, Doreen Valiente, Robert Hale, London, 1978

WITCHCRAFT: THE OLD RELIGION, Dr Leo Louis Martello, Citadel Press, Secausus, New Jersey, 1975

WITCHCRAFT, THE SIXTH SENSE, Justine Glass, Wilshire Book Company, Hollywood, California, 1965

A WITCHES BIBLE, VOLUME II, Janet and Stewart Farrar, Magickal Childe, New York, 1984

THE WITCHES' GODDESS, Janet and Stewart Farrar, Phoenix Publishing Company, Custer, Washington, 1987

THE WITCHES' QABALA, Ellen Cannon Reed, Llewellyn Publications, St. Paul, MN, 1986

THE WITCHES' WAY, Janet and Stewart Farrar, Robert Hale, London, 1984

WOMAN'S MYSTERIES, M. Esther Harding, Harper & Row, New York, 1971

Appendix Five:
Selected Essays And Columns

The following are columns and essays selected from among those written for a variety of neopagan and Wiccan newsletters and journals.

THE WITCH & THE CRONE

It was my fortune this past Solstice to take a journey to see the Crone. It was an exciting travel, for my years have been spent where soils are rich and brown, the fertility of land prepared by the passage of glaciers and the Mother Valley of the Mississippi. The winters bring us comforters of snow and the summers are filled with hot, sunny days and near-violent storms.

My departure from Los Angeles followed a private Solstice ritual, a rite taken in a temple of Mens' Mysteries. A special joy, for my Tradition embraces both Goddess and God as equal in Magick. Yet it prepared me for embarking across the desert, in wonder at the intensity of experience which must have awaited the early explorer, isolated with horse and countless days of desolate country.

My heart was amazingly uplifted in reaching the Arizonan mountains, at finding snow SNOW! and green-growing trees taller than a human head after a hundreds upon hundreds of miles of desert. The further into the desert, the more the bones of the Earth showed through, for this is the land of the Crone. Here She shows the passage of time, where a stone face wears the work of wind-blown sand and small, desert flora set roots into a time-worn crevice.

The Grand Canyon is the Valley of the Crone. Harsh, unrelenting, She is severe yet cradles within Her arms a love which tenders the blossoms springing forth when the seasons fall just so. Whereas Yellowstone awes one by the aliveness of the Earth bubbling and spewing forth, at the Canyon I found the stillness, the stark wonder of what has taken Ages to create. These are the means by which Mother Nature brings awe to the Wiccan Heart. To visit this great site is to fall even deeper in love with the Crone.

I am a Witch, and I take my religious journeys to see Her at work. Give me the choice between a Pagan festival and a natural wonder, and I will always go to meet the Mother. She alone has the power to balance the fierce powers which rage within my Saturnine being. She alone can balance the depth of devotion to this planet which She evokes in my heart. For the Wiccan, some of the greatest of religious sites in this country are those untouched by temple, but preserved by the intense hands of the Mother-At-Work, in all Her aspects.

7 February 1987

WHAT WILL HAPPEN WHEN YOU DIE?

What will happen to you when you die? In most of the United States, you are likely to undergo a Christian burial. I have seen this take place numerous times in recent years, yet when booking speaking engagements my requests to address issues of Death & Dying are generally met with dismay at such a morose and depressing topic. Such attitudes remind me too much of the reasons I left my childhood religion behind me. My religion of Wicca sees death as the counterpart to birth, each intrinsically linked in the beautiful and sensual Circle of Life. To consider death a topic inappropriate for Pagan Festivals is akin to slandering the Crone.

Neo-Paganism is very young and a major focus of my Priesthood is to do my part to wake up these young communities. These are the years we must do whatever legal work is necessary, whatever religious work is essential, and whatever work must be done to change our attitudes towards death. Death was considered a momentous adventure in most ancient Mystery Religions. The same should hold true today.

Wiccan beliefs often include reincarnation and the ability to reclaim our athames, Books of Shadows, and the like. This certainly is not going to happen if nothing has been done to assure that your group (church?) has the necessary provisions for such work. What can be done? Make certain you have a ceremony appropriate for that Initiatory occasion. It would be wise to do the paperwork to be legally incorporated as a Church. Simple non-profit status is very easy. Consider having a will which guarantees that your pagan religion is something which you will take with you at death. Do you really wish to be buried according to the rites of your parents? You would be shocked to discover that the laws of many states turn your body over to next-of-kin and I have even seen pagan spouses, when beset with grief, allow the Christian families to make all religious arrangements.

If you are ready to embrace death in a joyful way, it will not be necessary for the Crone to fight with you when the time has come. After all, She alone is the one best suited to teach you the best parts of which lead to birth.

18 March 1987

FOR THE SAKE OF ARGUMENT

There is a quiet debate which skirts the hem of many gatherings, arising from confusion over terminology. We are all quick to explain what it means to be pagan. The word Witchcraft or the word Wicca have numerous definitions, some of which may at best have highly questionable, archaic sources used as references. But I'd like to jump in feet first and state clearly and loudly that for a growing number of us, the words Wicca and pagan are NOT one and the same.

You may wonder why I do not capitalize the word pagan. I think of pagan as an adjective describing a lifestyle that may (or may not!) include pagan religions, no matter what culture they be derived from. Certainly at pagan gatherings the word is used as an adjective, but as a noun it has as much definition — or truly perhaps less — than the word Christian [capitalized, for that denominational label is based upon a proper name].

171

There are no singular unifying belief systems in neo-paganism. There is a general acceptance of the sacredness of the Earth, but such a belief is also found in a significant number of other religions and is not, in and of itself, a distinguishing characteristic. Among pagans there is no ritualistic cohesiveness (there is far moreso among Wiccans). Indeed, there are a substantial number of pagans who decry not only formal ritual, but see their rituals as synonymous with daily living and claim it their right to distrust any form of organized, group Circle. It is possible to make generalizations about pagans, but one must inevitably mention the exceptions.

Wicca, as a religious sect, denotes a far more specific belief system. It is Initiatory by nature, literate (having a Book of Shadows), concerned with educational goals (as in studying the Craft of the Wise), and works with remarkably similar ethics and creeds among the yet-diverse groups. This is not to say that many pagans are not literate and do not study, but paganism does not imply study and training as much as it does a mode of living.

The word Wicca is often treated as of sacred origin, though any competent historian or adept at syntax would quickly dispel those proofs. Regardless, the term denotes a reasonably specific religious tradition and belief. Its modern roots lie primarily in what are called the Gardnerian and the Alexandrian traditions implanted in the midst of the Twentieth Century and in all of the accompanying myths created in these modern times.

An essential concept I state in this article is that neither Wicca nor paganism is better than the other. Both are equally valid choices. All Wiccans are, arguably, pagans, but certainly not all pagans are Wiccan, which reminds me of the exercise in logic taught in secondary schools about fennecs and foxes . . .

12 October 1987

THE CRONE WALKS IN MY SHOES

I have wielded my athame with the moon for so many turnings of the Wheel that it has been drawn out into the lunar-shaped sickle of the Crone. I no longer play the games of Beltane nor leap through the Midsummer fires for I live with one foot perpetually in the Otherworld. I carry the Mysteries of Hallowmas with me at every Sabbat.

No longer do I shudder at the thought of death. In fact there are those days when I think of it as welcome, a comforter of down rather than a shroud. And I have grown far more tolerant of life, yet far more intolerant (and likely to wield the scythe) of intolerance and the treatment of life as being of little value.

The Crone walks in my shoes. S/he is far more than the third aspect of the Goddess. S/he is also Cronus, Saturn, Dread Lord of Death. And S/he is the voice of death and the gleeful humour which comes with age when one realizes that so much of what we once considered so very, very important truly isn't important at all.

And S/he walks quickly, now. Once I was a child and older people talked about the speed of time's gait. Now I sit in amazement as the Wheel of the Year turns like fortune's spinning wheel. And I have barely prepared to dread the worst of winter when the bulbs have resurrected themselves for Beltane. It goes fast and some day I may choose to spend a week reliving my favoured memories. Oh, you'll call me senile then, but I'll be having the best of times. For me it'll be an afternoon's reverie, for my youthful Moons passed more slowly and I'll be living in both worlds.

I love being old. I would not give to you a day of it. It is the most delicious of all of life's Mysteries. Sadness is no longer a consideration for I have seen too much. Daily sadness has melded into reality as much as daily joy. It is serenity which greets my morning. Death and birth are reality. The harshness and sometime-injustices of life are part of the continuum of life. It is the youth who hold fantasies of a perfect world and while those dreams are essential it is the old who know better. Life will always hold mixtures of good times and painful times, perhaps in varying proportions, but a mixture nonetheless.

Ah, the Crone stirs the pot. All of it. The hell I've seen, the hell I've raised and the hell I've caused. And the joys, the best orgasm (which carried me into infinity — ah, what a sweetie that one was!); the rites of passage, the birth I brought forth, the death I sat for. The Mother/Father stirs the cauldron to provide food. The Maiden and the Lad fill it with water and bob for apples, or fill it with flame and leap o'er the fiery tongues midst shrieks of glee. But I scribe my Circle with the sickle of time, now, and cook the mixture of life and death that I know reality to be. And that is the best cooking of all.

7 May 1987

THE TAO OF WICCA

I am of the wisdom of Mother Nature. I am the forces which churn and cleanse our glorious Planet Earth. I am in the eruption of a volcano, dancing in joy at the creation and birthing. I sing in the ferocity of a blizzard's wind, purifying and chasing life into the Underworld that it be born again at the Spring. I am the dry, quiet song of monotonous drought, for even fertility must be brought into balance and there is no place upon Earth which may be Eden for ever: all is to be recycled.

I live in all weather and I am of all things, for I am the Tao of Wicca. I live in the Mother's wisdom and She is wise. I am the patience and acceptance which allow me to dance to whichever music She desires to bring forth. She alone knows when She should sound rain's drum and She alone should determine the place. I am the sound of the tambourine She plays for Her hail. She alone knows which days should be given to honour the Sun and although you may desire to seek favour, such things are not in the domain of humans, nor should they be. To take water which rightfully belongs elsewhere on Earth is an invocation of a later drought, for there is balance in all things and one must never attempt to outguess what lies around the bend of time. Wise is the Wiccan who trusts that the Mother knows best the ways of weather.

There is beauty in all weather, even when She is attempting to enlighten you through monotony. Trust Her. The Mother is wise and you are but human. She is not the Tao but I live within Her. When She floods upon the face of the Earth it is but the lavage of an entity. And when the Crone stirs Her cauldron to the Music of Death, turn not to mourning, not to anger, but realize that She is but pruning in Her gardens in order that there be room for life and for growth. The Mother and the Crone are the same, and They garden to the music of the Tao.

23 December 1987

A GARDEN OF TRUST

For a gentle flower, it may be frightening to learn to trust. One must put away hurtful memories, be willing to be seen both at one's best and at one's worst. In learning to trust and to share with each other, you find yourself coming to terms with your ego, again and again.

The neopagan communities and those of the modern Witchcraft revival are surely a variety of individuals. In truth, we are as varied as the flowers in Mother Nature's gardens. We can only be brought to maturity when grown carefully from seed or already-established root stock. We must be strong and stable, attain the maturity of bud and then open, brought to bloom by both Sun and Moon.

We are like a botanical family. In our Ideals, we are all flowers, but in reality we might also have weedish tendencies. A weed is a flower disrespectful of others' space, spreading out into anothers' domain and attempting to perpetuate its own beliefs and existence at the expense of others.

All — flowers and weeds alike — are visited by the bees and other insects. This process might be thought of as akin to the sharing of ideas. The mind-to-mind interactions are like the

175

visits of the bees. Ideas can only make their presence known when the flower is opened to pollination.

To share this fertile garden of ours is also to observe and to encourage, to question and sometimes to provoke (and stir the soil!). There are those occasions when we must comfort, for no species is exempt from the crop-thinning blade of the Crone.

Establish your ability to trust over time. Be patient. Find those who are like you are and who like you for what you are. Although, at first glance, you might think that because we are all flowers we are all close family. Some of us are prickly, some wilt easily, some grow tall and cast a shadow upon others. Be wise unto your own being and learn more about these communities. You may not find your closest family in your own geographical area, for the nature of Aquarius is that we weave networks and communicate through wires and postal routes.

And on those days when it is most difficult to trust, take some time and move into yourself. The most important place in which to begin establishing trust is within the seed of your self.

4 July 1988

Appendix Six
Ritual Songs and Chants

The Chants of Lothlorien

Chants are frequently sung as rounds, the text repeated as a means of building the group's energy. Music is a known way of weaving the Magick of a working group.

> Bring all the Magick Together
> This is the song I sing . . .

One of my favorite chants, written in the winter of 1985-86, I affectionately call this my 'close encounters' chant. When sung as a four-part round, the harmony creates a chord that seems to stir a joyous vibration similar to that of the space vehicle in Spielberg's movie. The chord is an F-A-C with the G as a lowered seventh.

> Sing for the Springtime
> Sing for the rain,
> Sing for the Springtime
> Summer comes again . . .

As were almost all of the chants, this was written with the flash of inspiration, in which words and music arrive out of the inner wellspring as part of ritual sweeping. This chant was written in preparation for the Spring Equinox, although it has proven wonderful at any time when we wish to contemplate the turning The Wheel of the Year. It also can easily be sung as a four-part round.

> Bring the Sun King, bring the Sun King,
> Watch Him grow, watch Him grow,
> He will grow to Summer, He will grow to Summer,
> Then He'll go, then he'll go . . .

Every Book of Shadows ought have a chant which everyone can sing, regardless of the individuals' perceptions of their musical ability. The 1985 Yule Sabbat brought some fun words and this chant is, indeed, joyous. Since these words are set to one of the most popular rounds, it is easily woven into a four-part chant.

> We love the Goddess and we love our home,
> Make it safe by night and day.
> Fill it up with Magick, fill it up with love, oh
> This is the boon we pray.

Written for the house blessing of a Wiccan mother and her three pagan daughters, this chant can be sung as a round but takes a little more concentration. It is most effective when taken at a lively tempo, accompanied by bells, drums and rhythm instruments made by children!

> Heal our Sister name,
> Bring the Goddess, bring what may . . .
> Heal our Sister name,
> Bring the Horned One, bring what may . . .

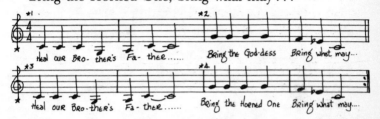

This chant is known in The Rowan Tree Church as the 'Healing Chant'. It makes a strong four-part round and has words which enable it to be adaptable for any person's name or relationship. The words sister and brother usually are sung in reference to the 'family' which exists as the Church membership but can easily be replaced by 'good friend' or other words. Of interest is the ethical approach to healing. Although we ask that the Universe promote healing, we also state that we accept the Universe's wisdom . . . . . 'Bring what may'. This chant dates to 1986 and has begun to spread among many other groups. Not only does this chant carry well in four-part but with enough strong singers can be expanded to eight-part, with one part begun at each measure.

> By fire and smoke do I invoke our
> Father from above . . .
> Fill this rite with Your might, with
> Sacredness and love . . .

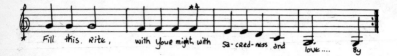

Fill this. Rite, with your might, with sa-cred-ness and love.... By

This four-part chant was written in 1987 as I set the song texts
of The Ritual of Lothlorien to music for the Yule ritual. If you
are wondering why all of my music dates from recent years, it
seems that a well-spring of ritual music was released within me
after I retired as a professional chamber musician.

> I will raise the cone of pow'r,
> I will invoke chance . . .
> I can dance the Witches' round,
> I will do the dance . . .

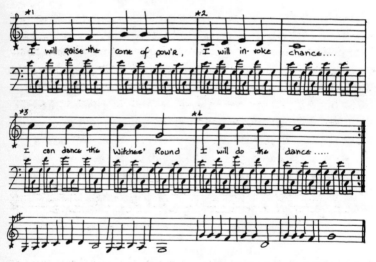

I am including the dulcimer part which accompanies the 'Cone
of Power' chant. One of the drawbacks of writing for a dulcimer
is that it 'lives' only in one key. This four-part chant may be a
little high for many voices but can easily be changed to the key
of G.

> Lord and Lady bless this Circle,
> Bring Thy children Home . . .

180

This chant was originally written for our First Degree Ritual of Initiation, sung by the Priest and Priestess as they carry the left and right altar candles (respectively) around the Circle. The word 'home' is chanted to be synonymous with the word Ohm. As one is chanting the Ohm, the other sings the moving line.

The next chant is one written while I was completing the manuscript for this very book. As Elder, I created a project for The Mystery School. We are combining the chants, invocations and various things that the students and College of Mentors collectively create and these are all being assembled into a Ritual for the celebration of morning, to be used in putting one's day into a Magickal perspective.

> I see the Sun rise,
> He's here to welcome in the day ...

There are also chants which do not readily lend themselves to round-singing. A fortunate group will find its members able to sing harmonies. The following chant has been written in a harmonic sense loosely based upon the blues. It was written in 1979 while walking to gather the morning mail for The Unicorn and for The Rowan Tree. Various names for the Goddess can easily be inserted and the melody sung over and over.

> Oh Goddess,

Oh Goddess,
Oh Goddess,
Come, come to me . . .

The next chant was written in 1986 for a Ritual which dealt with the AIDS crisis. Held at a beautiful city park, the ritual opened with a procession around a large pond. There were banners and drums and a feeling of strength which led my inspiration to bring forth this march:

Heal the Earth!
Heal the people!
Heal our planet tonight!

The following chant was originally written for the Hallows Rite in our Book of Shadows, but was found to be so useful in drawing the various threads of Goddess energy which have permeated so many cultures and peoples over the Ages that it is frequently included in The Ritual of Lothlorien.

Come Dear Goddess,
Come this night,
Join us in this Magick Rite

Following the first verse, the names of the Goddess create the next lines. As the final four lines of the chant are sung, the

tempo slows and the powers are brought to the Circle's centre
and focused.

> Come, Astoreth ...
> Come, O Ceres ...
> Come, O Freya ...
> Come, Demeter ...
> Come, Cerridwen ...
> Aphrodite ...
> Come, O Hertha ...
> Come, Hecate ...
> Come, Astarte ...
> Come, Arianrhod ...
> Come, Cardea ...
> Come, O Cybele ...
> Aradia ...
> Come, O Bridget ...
> Come, O Isis ...
> Come, Diana ...
> Come, Great Mother ...
> Come, Young Maiden ...
> Come, Old Woman ...
> Come, Great Goddess ...

The final chant included in this text is really more of a song,
although it can be sung in a round. It is almost ethereal when
voices blend in harmonies and countermelodies. The dulcimer
part is included with the melody.

> Light the candle ...
> Bring the fire ...
> Light the candle ...
> Sun grows higher ...

Community Traditions develop songs which become part of the culture and a means of expressing the symbols of the group. These songs are often incorporated into ritual work or gatherings and, in time, become part of the musical heritage of the Tradition. 'Meet Me In The Greenwood' is a song for the Priest to sing as he invokes Pan, as a prelude to the Great Rite.

Meet Me In The Greenwood
Meet Me in the Green-wood, to-night be-neath the Moon,
Watch Me dance on clo-ven hooves and lis-ten to My tune,
Let me dance the Ma-gick Round and sow you seeds of lust,
Gaze into My eyes, My sweet, and love Me as you must;

For You and I are one My love, re-flec-tions of the same;
And We both know the Song of Pan and we both know His
   Name.
So Meet Me in the woods to-night and make with Me sweet
   love,
To soar on ec-stasy's strong wings into the sky above.
Oh Meet Me in the Green-wood, to-night beneath the
   Moon.
Watch Me dance on clo-ven hooves and lis-ten to My tune.

'Join Me In the Woods' is a song I am particularly fond of singing prior to a Handfasting Ritual. While the lyrics can be interpreted as useful prior to the Great Rite, they also convey the essence of Perfect Love and Perfect Trust and the imagery useful in working within the astral temples of Lothlorien. Imagine a group of minds riding their Unicorn spirit guides to a stone Circle set in the astral reality.

The song opens with an instrumental introduction. As with the songs which follow, the text shows the manner in which the syllables change with the melody. The dulcimer part should be quite playable on many instruments.

Join Me In the Woods Tonight
Join me in the woods to-night and sail-ing go, my love . . .
We shall ride the La-dy's light, a wan-der-ing a-bove . . .
Up-on our steed, a U-ni-corn, we shall reach Her light . . .
Join me in the Moon, my love, and sail-ing go to-night.

Meet me in the Cir-cle where the stones are tall and
     strong . . .
Help me call the fire! the air! the wa-ter, earth in song . . .
To-geth-er we will dance the round and raise a pow'r so
     fair . . .
Per-fect Love and Per-fect Trust, tis gen-tle Mag-ick there.

Join me in the woods to-night and sail-ing go my love . . .
We shall ride the La-dy's light, a wan-der-ing a-bove . . .
For we shall raise a cone of pow'r to shim-mer in the
     night . . .
As we shall do for-ever love, in heart to heart de-light.

'She's Dying 'is a song written to assist in a protest against the treatment of our planet Earth. It was written for a solo voice singing the verses with everyone singing along on the chorus and on the two recurrent phrases in each of the verses, "Gone is our future", and "Have we all gone crazy?". Of all the music presented in this book, this is the only political song and has been written in such a manner that it may be used in any public situation.

Written in January, 1988, it is my hope that verses will continue to be added as this song is sung by increasing numbers of people who deeply care about out planet's future.

She's Dying
Oh, God, She's dy-ing . . . [*chorus*]
Oh, God, they're kill-ing Her . . .
Stop them! Why don't You stop them!
Be-fore it's too late, God,
Be-fore it's too late, God . . .
[*verses*]
Oh, the Wa-ter, sto-len, sold . . .
Filled with kill-ers, blood-y cold!
Gone is our fu-ture; What will the child-ren drink?
Have we gone cra-zy? What will our child-ren think?

Air, once pris-tine, pure and new . . .
Now is poi-soned, nev-er blue . . .
Gone is our fu-ture; How will our chil-dren live?
Have we gone cra-zy? Tis cer-tain death we give . . .

Peo-ple liv-ing ev'-ry-where . . .
There's no land left, none to care . . .
Gone is our fu-ture; We cut down all the trees.
Have we gone cra-zy? Poi-soned the birds and bees.

Soil for grow-ing, now is dead . . .
Filled with gar-bage, tox-ics, lead . . .
Gone is our fu-ture; Time pass-es quick, like sand.
Have we gone cra-zy? We must pre-serve our land.

See the leaves drop, dy-ing, brown . . .
A-cids rain-ing, fall-ing down.
Gone is our fu-ture; It will be des-ert land.
Have we gone cra-zy? We've turned our crops to sand.

Ba-by seals clubbed: coats to wear . . .
Hear the moth-ers scream and care . . .
Gone is our fu-ture; Who do we think we are?
Have we gone cra-zy? Have we lost all re-gard?

To finish the song She's Dying, the chorus may be sung a number of times. Easily divided into two parts, (the second part entering after eight measures), it makes a superb round.

Pan's Song
Neath the Moon-light un-der Sun,
Cir-cle round when work is done!
Clo-ven hooves up-on the night!
Let My Mag-ick bless your rite!

In the Wood-land, through the glade,
With the hope of prom-ise made.
Share the laugh-ter, this you must!
Learn of joy, of love and trust.

Hear My Mu-sic, hear My tune!

Lis-ten to the song of Moon,
The song of Sun, of fun and mirth.
Heed My call for I am Earth.

I am Pan, the Wood-land Song.
Dance My rhy-thms all night long.
Join Me as My pipes I play.
Chant-ing all your cares a-way.

The following is the music for the Circle-casting songs in the Ritual of Lothlorien. The melody for both the water cleansing and the salt blessing is the same, a further mingling of these two elements and has been written for voice and folk harp.

Be gone all dark-ness, flee this chal-ice.
Leave it free from evil mal-ice.
Fill it full with joy and love and
Bless-ings from the Gods a-bove.

Salt of the earth and salt of the sea.
Born of the pure so Bless-ed Be . . .
Water for bod-ies, salt for the soul.
At home in our Moth-er, such is our goal.

194

The following four songs are those sung by the Unicorns when they greet the Goddess in the Deva Ritual. In the Ritual of Lothlorien, this music enables the Priest/ess to sing the Goddess Songs when performing the ritual.

> O Beau-ti-ful La-dy,
> Gen-tle God-dess fair,
> Give to us Thy wis-dom,
> Fill us with Thine air!
> Bring to us Thy won-drous might,
> Gra-cious God-dess of the light!
> Ride the wings of Ra-pha-el and
> Bless this Mag-ick Rite!

Help us cast this Cir-cle and
Build a Mag-ick Ring.
Guide us to Your beau-ty our
Love to You we sing!
God-dess of the dawn-ing light,
Kiss the dew of morn-ing's sight!
Light the can-dle, ring the bell and
Bless this Mag-ick rite.

Great-est God-dess of the fire . . .
Fill my heart with Your de-sire . . .
Keep my feet upon Thy path . . .
Fill my heart with mirth and laugh . . .
Great-est God-dess, burn-ing bright . . .
Keep me in Thy Mag-ick Might . . .
Dance around the fi-re bright . . .
Chant the song and do the rite . . .

Fire burn-ing, fire bright . . .
Give my soul your Mag-ick light . . .
Help me rise a-new each day . . .
Keep me in Our La-dy's way . . .

197

Queen of the wa-ters, spark-ling in the Moon-light,
La-dy of the Heav-ens, danc-ing in the stars bright.
Dance in the laugh-ing waves, Call upon the Moon.
Cast the Cir-cle, chant the song. God-dess grant this boon.

Take us to Thy home-land, deep with-in the sea.
Bring the Moon in-to my heart, Dear Mo-ther, Bless-ed Be!
Dance in the laugh-ing waves, Call upon the Moon.
Cast the Cir-cle, chant the song. God-dess grant this boon.

Walk-ing on the Earth this day, sens-ing life with-in.
Liv-ing with the God-dess' song, we are free from sin!
Danc-ing in the for-est, chant-ing with the trees,
Cast-ing Mag-ick Cir-cles, Sing-ing Bless-ed Be's!

Moth-er of the Har-vest, God-dess of the fields,
You Who bring our dreams to ripe, You Who bless the yields,
Join us danc-ing in the wood, hear us sing-ing to the trees,
Help us cast our Circles, Hear our Bless-ed Be!

Appendix Seven:
The Deva Ritual of Lothlorien

And it came to pass that the Mother knew it was time. Yearly She tended the growing things in Her gardens, as She was Mother to all of Terra Firma. Flowers bloomed in Her honour. Trees grew tall with pride at being in Her touch; and the herbes paid heed to the cosmic dances, each growing wise in the music sung into their hearts in the days of the Ghyleana.

Each had grown in wisdom, and the Mother knew it was time to initiate the Herbe Devas into the Priest/esshood of the healers. It had come time to pass the knowledge of the herbes into the land, which lore is only for those who know Her greatest Mystery.

As the Moon waxed into fullness, all knowing was set ready and the night She fulfilled the waxing, all creatures gathered in the Land of Lothlorien, famed for its gardens and rivers.

The Herbe Devas, as chosen children of the Goddess, made clear a space on the sandy shores of a sacred river, deep within a glade. This site was special, for there grew no plants on this sand and all the creatures could frolic and play.

At the moment the Moon spilled Her light direct from overhead, a hush filled the world. One by one the stars began their ancient hymn and, as if out of the void, appeared the Goddess, riding a graceful Unicorn the same colour as the Moon.

The Lady stood at the centre of them all and spoke:

'I am the Mother of all and this world is the place of My altar. Here shall I bring My children and give unto them My greatest gift. They have prepared themselves, filled themselves with love and joy; yet they have studied the healing arts and learned to observe the celestial clock, the song of the Universe.

'Tonight will the Universe sing in love the miracle of being and on this night I will teach you the Greatest Mystery.'

The Devas gathered round Her, at the edge of a Circle. As they held hands, they felt the oneness of love flow through them, sunwise round the Lady.

Behind the Devas were all the creatures, sylphs, salamanders, all sorts of magickal beings, many of whom were bearing gifts.

Silence.

Nothing moved.

The Mother set Her tools upon the altar, set so She could smile upon the Earth as She sang her sacred songs.

She lit a candle, the left of the pair. The Devas nodded their heads, for they knew it was a symbol of the Sun, for He is the candle at Her sacred altar.

And She carried the flame to the right candle, as the Sun carries His light to the Moon.

All eyes watched Her create a sacred place.

Taking up a chalice of water, She cleansed it and sang this verse:

> Be gone all darkness,
> Flee this chalice,
> Leave it free from
> Evil malice.
> Fill it full with
> Joy and love and
> Blessings from the
> Gods above.

It brought tears to the eyes of the undines, who had brought the gift of water. They were very moved to share in this ritual. Next She held a bowl of salt, which had been the offering of the gnomes.

> Salt of the Earth,

> Salt of the Sea,
> Born of the Pure,
> So Blessed Be!
> Water for bodies,
> Salt for the soul,
> At home in your Mother,
> Such is your goal.

Gently She took three sprinkles of salt and mingled them into the vessel of water. Walking to the East, She aspurged a sacred circle, cleansing the space. She was delicate in the moonlight, dancing sunwise with the Deva-song of love. Droplets of holy water landed around the Circle, making the sacred ground ready.

The sylphs and salamanders were excited as She returned to the altar. Then, taking up their gifts of burning charcoal and the finest incense, She sprinkled the resins upon the coal and as the smoke wafted in a gentle breeze, carrying the scent to all, She held a thurible high, for all to see, and sang out:

> By fire and smoke do I invoke
> Your Father from above.
> Fill this rite with His might,
> With sacredness and love.

Even though the Sun God was at rest, for the Mother was at Her time, was He there, His essence in the sacred scent.

Now, as the space had been consecrated with all four elements, She sought to dance around Her Circle in great delight, first taking round the incense to share with all its fragrance, then Her magick wand to seal Her Blessing.

Eyes were wide at watching the Goddess at work, bringing the miracle of love into all hearts. She walked to the East, and drawing a magick blade from an inner pocket of Her gossamer robe, scribed a large, five-pointed star in the air and called out:

> Lords of the East!

Creatures of Air!
Come watch this rite!
Bring blessings fair!
Sylphs and swords and dawn's fair light;
Where the rainbow's born;
Raphael, on Eurus' breath,
Will ride the wings of morn . . .

As Her words sang into the night, a Unicorn the colour of the breeze flew in on large, pale yellow wings. Kneeling in the East before Her, he said,

Oh Beautiful Lady,
Gentle Goddess fair,
Give to us Thy wisdom,
Fill us with Thine air!
Bring to us Thy wondrous might,
Gracious Goddess of the light,
Ride the wings of Raphael
And bless this Magick Rite!
Help us cast this Circle
And build a magick ring!
Guide us to your beauty,
Our love to You we sing . . .
Goddess of the dawning light,
Kiss the dew of morning's sight!
Light the candle, ring the bell
And bless this Magick Rite!

And then Raphael, for that was the Unicorn's name, spoke of wisdom to the Devas as the Mother lit a candle the colour of his wings:

'And the Goddess breathed into the void, and behold, the gentle breezes caressed the soul of the Universe. Thus was born the essence of light, of laughter and cheer.

'Pan sat alone in the Mother's Woodland. Raising His pipes to his mouth, He brought forth the first music, the wings of song, floating in the airs . . .

'May the gentle winds of faith stir your souls into seeking the Mother. As the morning song of the dawning creeps over the horizon of your life, may we all share in the laughing and joy of wisdom; and may we float in the winged clouds of eternity . . .'

She strode to the South, brilliantly radiating joy and stretching Her arm into the sky, scribed a large pentagram, Her voice carrying strongly:

> Lords of the South!
> Creatures of Fire!
> Come, watch this rite!
> Bring us desire!
> Salamanders of the South;
> Notus' fiery breath.
> Living under Michael's care,
> Rebirth follows death . . .

A large Unicorn, the colour of flame, sprang out of nowhere. The Devas gasped. The Unicorn lowered its head and spoke to Her:

> Greatest Goddess of the fire,
> Fill my heart with Your desire.
> Keep my feet upon Thy path,
> Fill my heart with mirth and laugh!
> Greatest Goddess burning bright,
> Keep me in Thy magick might.
> Dance around the fire bright,
> Chant the song and do the rite.
> Fire burning, fire bright
> Give my soul your magick light,
> Help me rise anew each day,
> Keep me in Our Lady's Way.

Michael turned to the plant Devas. They listened closely as he spoke:

'From the warmth of Her maternal goodness did She bring fire to her children, to kindle in them the sparks of knowledge and the fires of delight . . .

'From the Sun we take our warmth, from our Mother comes desire. As the Phoenix rises, renewed of flames, may we, too, embrace the life beyond this.

'Our Eternal Goddess is the Cauldron of Cerridwen; may we dance around Her fires in eternal joy . . . May we embrace the fires of learning and kindle within our passion for wisdom.'

And the red candle She lit in the South as Michael spoke flamed brightly. Long, flowing steps brought Her to the West; and gracefully She carved a star into the night, singing out:

> Lords of the West,
> Creatures of Seas!
> Come, watch this rite,
> Fill it with ease!
> Creatures of the moonlit sea,
> Zephrus, undines all . . .
> Drink with love from Gabriel's cup,
> Hear your Goddess' call . . .

A beautiful, blue Unicorn, the colour of a clear mountain spring spilled out of the moon-filled night on widespread wings, and landed gently before Her with bowed head to say:

> Queen of the Waters,
> Sparkling in the moonlight,
> Lady of the Heavens,
> Dancing in the stars bright;
> Dance in the laughing waves,
> Call upon the Moon;
> Cast the Circle, chant the song,
> Goddess, grant this boon!
> Take us to Thy homeland,

Deep within the sea!
Bring the Moon into my heart,
Dear Mother, Blessed Be!
Dance in the laughing waves,
Call upon the Moon,
Cast the Circle, chant the song,
Goddess, grant this boon!

Seeing their Goddess dance and sparkle to the Unicorn's song brought dew to the eyes of the Devas. More than one eye brought forth a tear as the Unicorn, Gabriel, spoke these words unto them:

'From the deep waters of Her eternal wisdom, brings She forth the Mystery of Life; and thus does the Initiate take on the Quest of All-Knowing . . .

'From the Cauldron of Cerridwen we take compassion and love. Moving deep within the Mysteries we seek inner knowledge . . . May the God Neptune watch over the seeker as the Initiate plunges to the depths of knowing . . .

'Our Mother is the Moon's reflection upon rippling waters . . . May we eternally be bathed in Her love . . . May we seek Her calm, Her tranquility, as we travel from shore to distant shore . . .

The Mother walked to the North and, smiling upon the Earth, She raised Her blade and drew a brilliant pentagram into the air; and this call came from Her heart:

Lords of the North!
Creatures of Earth!
Come, watch this rite!
Fill it with mirth!
Gnomes and dryads, stones and trees,
Pentacles and Boreas' strength;
Auriel sends us wintertime
And nights of growing length!

At this, a Unicorn strode out of the forest. The colour of leaves,

Auriel trotted up on hooves that shone the hue of fresh-turned earth. Her eyes sparkled as if of moonlit snow as she bowed gently before the Lady to sing her greeting:

> Walking on the Earth this day,
> Sensing life within,
> Living with the Goddess' song,
> We are free from sin!
> Dancing in the forest,
> Chanting in the trees,
> Casting Magick Circles,
> Singing Blessed Be's!
> Mother of the harvest,
> Goddess of the fields,
> You Who bring our dreams to ripe,
> You Who bless the yields,
> Join us dancing in the wood,
> Hear us singing to the trees,
> Help us cast our Circle,
> Hear our Blessed Be's!

Although the Devas felt carried by Auriel's song nearly into dance, they stayed rooted to the spot and listened to the wisdom the Unicorn spoke of in her charge:

'In our quest for knowledge we cross the fields of the Earth-Mother and play in Her forests ... Her pulse is in the gardens, Her dance is in the jungles and from deep within Her springs knowledge as the fruits of the Earth ...

'Slowly She dances the seasonal rhythms, to the gentle music of the Woodlands. Pan plays upon His pipes and She dances, in the grasses, among the trees, to the Tune of the Gentle Hunter.

'Our Mother is the Earth and we are Her children. She gives us wisdom. may we seek Her knowledge in the flowers and in the green things ... And in the passing of time, when we give to Her our souls, She will take our bodies and plant them for Her flowers ...'

Almost without knowing, the Devas began to slowly dance round the Goddess, moving as the Sun dances with the Earth. Faster and faster they went, forming a dance of love, of joy and truth. The Unicorns stood alert, Guardians of the Magick, and the Lady smiled upon all that moved around Her.

Raising Her arms, She began a holy song, a song of love and creativity, a song of the fertility of the Earth. Calling out into the soul of nature, She sought Pan with Her music, to aid Her in teaching the Mystery.

The dryads were among the few who had seen the sight which now appeared. Horns like a woodland being, small delicate hooves that seemed always to dance, curls of fur thick upon His legs, a Woodland God sprang over the heads of the creatures as He joined the Lady.

Faster danced the Devas.

Pan and the Lady held hands and danced round and round in the moonlight, and for all who wondered Who He was, He sang this chant:

> Neath the Moonlight, under Sun,
> Circle round when work is done!
> Cloven hooves upon the night,
> Let My magick bless your rite!
> In the woodland, through the glade,
> With the hope of promise made,
> Share the laughter, this you must;
> Learn of joy, of love and trust!
> Hear My Music, hear My tune,
> Listen to the song of Moon,
> The song of Sun, of fun and mirth,
> Heed My call, for I am Earth!
> I am Pan, the Woodland Song.
> Dance My rhythms all night long.
> Join Me as My pipes I play,
> Chanting all your cares away.

Soon, all were dancing round and round, the gnomes taking

short, bounding steps, undines flowing gracefully. Griffins, dragouns, all danced and danced until it seemed the songs and love reached up to the Moon.

Again silence.

Pan and the Lady brought forth a large cauldron, filled with water, and set it in the centre of the Circle. When She nodded, a large dragoun, the colour of gold, stepped up from the South and breathed the kindling underneath into flame.

The Devas trembled. Fire was feared in the land, though they knew they would follow Her, even unto death.

All the Devas gathered before Her. The night was silent. Even the elves were still, for this night would exist but once in all eternity. The Devas all knelt. One by one they were touched by Her magick sword, then by Her lips as She kissed each upon the forehead. Assured, calm, they all knew they were truly ready for Initiation into the Priest/esshood. As if She heard their thoughts, She spoke:

'Then you shall be taught to be wise, so in the fullness of time you shall count yourselves among those who serve the Ancient Ones;

'And you shall grow to love the Music of the Woodland, to dance to the sound of His pipes, in step with cloven hooves and the forest song . . .

'And you shall learn the mystery of rebirth, filling your hearts with My Moonlight, growing in harmony with the Earth as Her children, protective of your Mother . . .

'And you shall grow in wisdom . . .

'And you shall grow in compassion . . .

'And in love shall you heal the sick, pursuing the arts of healing, the lore of the Mother's herbes, learning the psychic arts to cure, to nurture, to help Her children grow.

'And in wisdom you shall give counsel, knowing skills of divination, seeing how the children best flow in Universal Harmony, understanding planetary cycles and knowing prophecy.

'Thus will you be the Wise Ones, knowing the lores of Nature; of the heaths and of the country side, knowing all are One to the Mother, knowing all are One to the Father . . .'

One by one the Devas came forward. Each knelt and received the blessing:

'Let thy life and the life to come be in the service of the Lord and Lady . . .'

And then the Devas were taken up by Pan and the Goddess and placed into the boiling cauldron. There was no sadness, no fear, for being carried into the cauldron by both Mother and Father, they would come to understand the Greatest Mystery of Being: All is immortal, for all is born of the Great Mother of all Being.

The night burst into song and as Pan and the Lady stirred the cauldron, the Earth was filled with Magick. Lillies bloomed; flowers sparkled in the night. All was filled with the miracle of life which sprang from the cauldron between the Two.

Then, the fire tiring into coals, the cauldron was tipped and the broth, the Elixer of Life, poured forth. Wherever it touched the Earth, healing herbes sprang into being: Priests and Priestesses of the Devas; and in legends written of this night it is also said that humankind was born of this dew of the God and Goddess.

The Goddess again walked up to each Unicorn, beginning first with Raphael and, taking up Her blade, banished the pentagrams and bade all good even.

All the creatures turned into the night, seeking their homes and loved ones.

Pan and the Goddess sat alone and lay beneath the moonlight, sharing songs of love. This was the Magick of the Night, and They felt joyous together and danced, and played in delight until the dawn when the Lady took the sinking Moon, wrapped it in Her robes, and sailed into the stars upon Her Unicorn.

Pan took up His pipes and played the Sun into dawn-song.

All life upon the Earth was good.

Appendix Eight
Resources

Resources of Interest

Please keep in mind, when contacting the following, that the current neo-pagan communities and their publications do not always remain in existence for an indefinite period of time. It is likely that some of the publications listed below will no longer be functional when you make your inquiry. For that reason, make certain that your return address is extremely legible upon the envelope.

When requesting information on subscription rates or on the organization's policy about receiving a sample issue (for some there is a charge, for others not), enclose a business size envelope, stamped and addressed (clearly) to yourself. The following list is partial addendum of newsletters in print and does not attempt to express any favoritism.

AQUARIAN ARROW, BCM-OPAL, London, WC1N 3XX, England

THE BARD, 5102 N. 16th Dr. 3, Phoenix, AZ 85015

THE CAULDRON, c/o Mike Howard, 4 Llysonnen Cottages, LLysonnen Rd., Meidim, Carmathen, Dyfed, Wales

CIRCLE NETWORK NEWS, PO Box 219, Mt. Horeb, WI 53572

COMPOST, c/o V. Walker, 729 Fifth Ave., San Francisco, CA 94118

CONVERGING PATHS, PO Box 63-C, Mt. Horeb, WI 53572

FACTSHEET FIVE, c/o M. Gunderloy, 6 Arizona Ave., Rensselaer, NY 12144

THE GEORGIAN, 1908 Verde, Bakersfield, CA 93304

GOLDEN ISIS, PO Box 726. Salem, MA 01970

HARVEST, PO Box 228, S. Framingham, MA 01701

THE HIDDEN PATH, Windwalker, Box 891, Park Forest, IL 60466

IRON MOUNTAIN, PO Box 227, Florence, CO 81226
K A M, PO Box 2513, Kensington, MD 20895
THE LITTLEST UNICORN, PO Box 8814, Minneapolis, MN 55408
MAGICAL BLEND, PO Box 11303, San Francisco, CA 94101
OPEC NEWS, PO Box 605, Springdale, AR 72764
PAGANA, PO Box 9494, San Jose, CA 95157
PALLAS SOCIETY NEWS, 1800 S. Robertson Blvd., Box 2105, Los Angeles, CA 90035
PANEGYRIA, PO Box 57, Index, WA 98256
RFD, Rt. 1., Box 127-E, Bakersville, NC 28705
SHADOWPLAY, PO Box 343, Petersham, NSW 2039, Australia
SHETOTEM, PO Box 27465, San Antonio, TX 78227
STARDUST SALAMANDER, PO Box 75, Tunas, MO 65764
THESMAPHORIA, 5856 College Ave., Oakland, CA 94618
THE UNICORN, PO Box 8814, Minneapolis, MN 55408
WICCAN REDE, PO Box 473 c/o Morgans and Merlin, 3700 Al Zeist Holland
THE WHITE LIGHT, Box 93124, Pasadena, CA 91109
WILDFIRE, PO Box 9167, Spokane, WA 99209
YGGDRASIL, c/o P. Priest, 537 Jones St., 165, San Francisco, CA 94102

The following organizations are the more public in providing networking, study or other resources which may be of interest to the Wiccan student:
Circle Sanctuary, PO Box 219, Mt. Horeb, WI 53572
Covenant of the Goddess, Box 60151, Chicago, IL 60660
Fellowship of Isis, Clonegal Castle, Clonegal, Enniscorthy, Eire (Ireland)
Our Lady of Enchantment, PO Box 1366, Nashua, NH 03061
The Pallas Society, PO Box 18211, Encino, CA 91316
The Rowan Tree Church, PO Box 8814, Minneapolis, MN 55408 Within which is The Mystery School described in this text.
Frost's School of Wicca, PO Box 1502, New Bern, SC 28560